EDITED BY

THE CALIFORNIA REVOLUTION

CAREY McWILLIAMS

GROSSMAN PUBLISHERS · New York

The 1968 New York University Book
Publishing Workshop participated in the
preparation and production of this book.

CONTENTS

INTRODUCTION
Carey McWilliams

The simplest, least disputable thing to say about California, now our most populous state, is that it is, and always has been, a revolution—a revolution that has been accelerating in recent years. As a state it sprang into being overnight. California, as Lord Bryce said, grew "like a gourd in the night." With the discovery of gold the westward movement of population became a stampede to California; thousands of migrants came round the Horn, over the Isthmus, and across the plains. Those who came by land "leapfrogged" over the intermountain West. As might be expected, the California Gold Rush was not simply another "gold rush"; it was, and remains in retrospect, *the* Gold Rush, unique in the annals of mining "strikes" and "rushes." For one thing, it was perhaps the first—and the last—"poor man's gold rush" in history; there was little law and order, land titles were virtually non-existent, and the gold was there, in the creeks, to be panned by those who first arrived on the scene. And the consequences were, of course, unique. In California, wrote Blake Ross, "the energy of an expanding frontier met the energy released by the discovery of gold . . . [and] California became a great golden crucible that held within its mountainous rim all the elements of a new kind of American life. . . . [Here] for a few short years, man was nearly free of the incubus of the past." Later, after the 1860s, the past closed in, or seemed to, but only for a time and subsequent "booms" and "discoveries," of various kinds, regenerated the old energies, exuberance, and sense of freedom. This intimation of being nearly able to shake free of the incubus of the past and move, as by a giant step, into the future has always been widespread and deep-rooted. A potent myth, it has been responsible for the extravagant expectations, odd emanations, and almost messianic enthusiasms that many observers have noted over so many years. It has been, and is, a quality that Californians *feel*. "Here," as the poet Hildegarde Flanner wrote of California, "is a centering of human energy and desire . . . it may be that the quality of life has here more of future and hope and excitement, as well as more uncertainty, than in some countries long settled and not constantly changing."

Rapid, revolutionary change is the story of California and the pace of change has been accelerating. A truly extraordinary variety of factors—social, cultural, environmental—have interacted in California in such a way as to enable the state to maintain, with occasional slow-downs, its original momentum. Just as the energies released by the discovery of gold put California into orbit with one mighty blast-off, so it has been kept spinning, faster and faster, by a succession of subsequent, providentially timed discoveries and "explosions" of one kind or another: the "green gold" of lettuce and other produce crops, which made it the truck garden of America; the "black gold" of oil; motion pictures, tourism, the aerospace industry. In the century that has elapsed since the discovery of gold, California has raced through the familiar evolutionary cultural cycle—pastoral, agricultural, industrial, post-industrial—with a speed that has probably modified the processes involved. The range and variety of the state's resources is legendary but, from an early date, the unlocking of many of these resources has required an advanced technology (see the chapter by Howard F. Gregor) which in turn has added greatly to its wealth and power. Geographic position has been a major factor. California, for example, is the keystone to a thirteen-state western distribution area, extending eastward to the Rockies and westward into the Pacific trading area. "What America is to Europe," wrote Lord Bryce, "what Western America is to Eastern, that California is to the other Western states. . . . [It is] the last place in the West before you come to Japan." The state's indebtedness to certain early immigrant groups (the Chinese and Japanese) who, reversing the familiar migration pattern, crossed the Pacific to settle there, can never be fairly or fully calculated. Climate, atmosphere, and geographic position have combined to bring about highly important but quite unforeseen latter-day developments. For example, the Mt. Wilson and Palomar observatories are not located in Southern California by chance; nor are the motion picture and aerospace industries mere accidents of historical development.

For years a vague consensus has prevailed—for which reasons are seldom cited—that California is a pace-setter for the rest of the country, a place of innovation and experimentation. Revolutions, of course, are compelled to experiment, and the absence or weakening of traditional restraints makes it possible for them to do so. In California, the predisposition to innovate and experiment is primarily to be explained as a response to special needs and challenges; as elsewhere, necessity has been the mother of invention. At one time, for example, California boasted a thriving farm-machinery industry because local conditions required special implements. There are, of course, other reasons, some of which I have touched on elsewhere (see *Southern California: An Island on the Land,* 1946; *California: The Great Exception,* 1951; and a paper included in *The Cultural Arts,* University of California, 1964, p. 77). But when all is said and done, one is left with a feeling that most of the explanations which have been advanced fail to touch on an essential element. An elusive, intangible factor has been overlooked, perhaps because it cannot be precisely defined. There is something in the atmosphere of the state that not merely stimulates the demand for "something better" but creates the market for it and the means to provide it. And not only in products, homes, and facilities. Today, for example, California has the most generously supported if not necessarily the best educational system in the world (see the chapters by Mel Wax and James P. Degnan). Californians want "a better life"; they expect it, they think it is their right, they are convinced it is attainable, and they are prepared to pay for it.

Somewhat related to this same feeling or social attitude is the persistent pursuit of utopias of all kinds: the early utopian settlements, the retirement colonies, the first "colony" communities (as where a group of families, of the same religious persuasion, would pick up bag and baggage and resettle in California), and such special, and fascinating, utopias as Kaweah, Krotona, Point Loma, Llano del Rio. The same impulse carries over into the present. Nowadays "instant cities" are built for special groups, as subdivisions were once laid out for them (see the chapter by Theodore Roszak), and the persistent "cultism" of earlier periods finds expression in today's "awareness cults." California, in fact, has always been utopia-prone, always impatient, as Lord Bryce said, of the slow approach of the millenium, always ready to "try violent, even if perilous, remedies for a present evil." Hence Kearneyism (in the 1870s), George-ism, Townsendism, the Epic Movement, the Utopian Society, Ham-'N'-Eggs ($30 Every Thursday), and other isms, including "dianetics." The politics of the state (see the chapter by Gladwin Hill) have always been, to put it mildly, somewhat volatile. But in these, as in so many other respects, California is not so much different from the rest of the country as it is "more so." As far back as 1883, a writer in the *Overland Monthly* got this aspect of the state's social and political life just right. California, he said, "is in almost every respect an intensification of the American spirit . . . only more so." But one must concede that in the prodigiously fertile environment of California—particularly in Southern California—this innocent phrase, "only more so," can take on some rather alarming dimensions. In California geraniums are tall and sturdy as small trees, sugar beets are the size of watermelons, and, on the same scale, the bigots, fakirs, con men (the late C. C. Julian), prophets, and visionaries are giant-size.

Legend (the notion of California as the pot of gold at the rainbow's end) and climate (including atmosphere and setting, the quality of the light, the variation and contrast of light and shade) have had as much to do with stimulating migration to California as economic factors (see the article by Edward L. Ullman in *The Geographical Review*, January, 1954). And the difference in motivation has carried over into the everyday life of the Californians. Let's face it: certain regions of America are simply not imbued with the spirit of the amenities—North Dakota, for example. But the first California residents *knew* that Santa Barbara, Carmel, and Berkeley would one day be centers of art and learning, and the certainty has functioned down the years as a self-fulfilling prophecy. There has always been something in the atmosphere and setting that has invited leisure, the amenities, the arts. Years ago an observer pointed out that California could easily turn into "a land of sybarites." He should visit it today: John Morgan, the BBC producer, has said of the Californians that they have "seen the future and it plays." Many readers of Howard Taubman's feature article in *The New York Times*, January 3, 1967, were no doubt surprised by the caption: "Arts on West Coast: Challenge to East." But there is no occasion for surprise, really. The San Francisco theater of the Gold Rush, opera included, and the writing and publishing of that extraordinary decade before the completion of the Central Pacific Railroad, provided a preview of the future. Today California is on a "cultural" binge, some of it phony, some of it real (see the chapter by James Schevill), but all of it at one time or another predicted. In January, 1904, in conversation with George Sterling in San Francisco, William Butler Yeats, speaking of his visit to the States, said of California: "Here, if anywhere, I seem to hear the footsteps of the muses."

Today, of course, awareness of the California Revolution is worldwide. Not long ago the BBC, desiring to project a vision of the twenty-first century, presented a television documentary, directed by John Morgan, entitled *California: Year 2000.* In commenting on the film, some columnists came up with better titles: *Our California Future* was one, *California Is the Future,* another. Mr. Morgan says that he selected California as the inevitable locale because it is the center of the world's most advanced technology. By his reckoning, the state has 20,000 computers, some of which are already as obsolete as a Model T Ford. In the film, a computer expert, Dr. Tom Paine, expounds on miniaturization "with as much fervour as his namesake preached the Rights of Man." The film suggests that computers, guiding a sophisticated technology, will take over entirely from management staffs and factory production lines. People will begin to work at age twenty-five, they will work a three-day week, and retire at age fifty; in between they will take, at intervals, six-month vacations. Some of the British press comment is illuminating. Marsland Gander of the *Daily Telegraph* wrote: "During my visits to California I have been alternately elated and oppressed by its sunny, swirling gaiety, its opulent mad modernity." While the London *Times* offered this sedate comment: "California by the end of the century is going to be almost unrecognizable even from the place it is now." Correct. But Nancy Banks-Smith, of *The Sun,* obviously appalled by the prevision of the future which she had seen, wrote: "With a spot of luck, I hope to die before it happens!" More to the point were John Gross's comments in *The Observer:* "In California the contradictions of American life—or should it be of human nature?—seem to glare twice as fiercely as anywhere else. The most technologically advanced area in the world, it may shortly be governed by Ronald Reagan (alas, it now is—C. McW.)." The laboratory of the future, it can *still* produce a bang like the Watts riot. In Palo Alto, seven-year-olds are being trained to use computers; in San Francisco, psychiatrists report that "more and more it is machines which stalk through their patients' nightmares." True, all too true, and the contradictions will not abate for a long time to come because the revolution continues. An awareness of the contradictions is, in fact, clearly reflected in the anticipations of the Californians. "Onward California's Millions," wrote Art Seidenbaum in a 1967 New Year's piece in the Los Angeles *Times* but he promptly added, as a cautious after thought, "And Upward?" The magazine *Los Angeles,* in a 1967 forecast, took a schizophrenic view of the future. Jim Murray, in a lead article entitled "I'll Get Off Here If You Don't Mind!" wanted no part of a future California "sprayed with pesticide, fungicide, fertilized, irrigated, paved, bulldozed, urbanized, depersonalized, treeless, streamless, with sepulchral cities and bloodless people." But the editors were quite sanguine, pointing out that "the fantasies of only a few decades ago have become truth and the fantasies of today have the ring of future truth." Indeed preoccupation with the future is a special aspect of a persistent tendency in California to transpose illusion and reality. The creation of illusions is one of the state's major industries (see the chapter by John Bright).

Ambivalent attitudes—fascination and revulsion, elation and concern, enthusiasm and misgivings—have always characterized reactions to California and for a good reason. Revolutions have their destructive aspects. Sometimes the damage they cause is irreparable. The acceleration of the California Revolution during the postwar years has ravaged the landscape, ripped out orchards, and caused no end of needless damage and mindless destruction (see Richard G. Lillard's chapter on what has happened to California agriculture). If new and often exciting social patterns and institutions are forever emerging in California, old idea patterns and obsolete institutions are forever dying. The state ranks first in social inventiveness (see Jennifer Cross's chapter) and also, unhappily, in certain forms of social pathology. This, too, has always been the case. And for this contradiction there is, of course, an explanation. It has been repeatedly noted that new settlers in remote areas often develop a morbid consciousness of the "destiny" of the region; they become more nationalistic than they were before they resettled and definitely more so than the residents of the older areas of settlement from which they came. At the same time the new home is so different from the old that it often generates an intense nostalgia for the past and a paranoid fear of the future. Migrants to regions which have no settled social or institutional life—in which the steadying effect of custom and tradition is weak—tend to be extremely self-conscious. In such areas the spotlight of social acceptance or rejection focuses on the groups which are unable to join *quickly* the developing amalgam. Not certain just who is who—in fact nobody knows just who is who in such areas—the latest migrants will usually seek to identify with the socially dominant groups. New residents in Northern California communities are no more reactionary than old residents; but in Southern California, where the dominant elements have been until recently quite conservative, the new residents try to outdo the old, as by forming chapters of the John Birch Society (see *"The Political Cultures of California"* by Raymond E. Wolfinger and Fred I. Greenstein, Stanford University, November, 1966).

The kind of tensions generated between old and new residents accounts, in part, for some of the contradictions in West Coast politics. Dr. Earl Pomeroy, in his excellent volume, *The Pacific Slope* (1965, p. 216) notes that Woodrow Wilson, speaking in

New Jersey in 1911, said that he looked to the West Coast for inspiration and leadership in the progressive movement; the laws of Oregon, he said, "point the direction which we must also take." And indeed California and Oregon—and to a lesser extent Washington—did provide models of what was once regarded as "progressive legislation." But as Pomeroy goes on to say, "as rapidly as the coast and its leaders built their reputation for progressivism, they lost it." If the Progressive Movement was strong in California and Oregon, the Ku Klux Klan was notably strong in both states in the 1920s. The progressivism of Hiram Johnson, Culbert Olson, Earl Warren, and Edmund G. Brown represents one side of the tradition (the older, more free-wheeling, liberal side); the regimes of Friend Richardson, Frank Merriam, and now Ronald Reagan represent the "fundamentalist" aspect which has usually found strong support among new residents. Contrasting types, of all sorts, are certainly not uncommon in California. In the history of California journalism such names as Fremont Older and Lincoln Steffens can be paired with Joe Knowland and William Randolph Hearst. Since California is like the rest of the country "only more so," it is not surprising that, within the state, the extreme types to be found in national life are more numerous and more "extreme" than elsewhere. This creates within the state sharp clashes and divisions and glaring contrasts. Such a picturesque character as the late Colonel Charles Erskine Scott Wood might be said to represent the libertarian tradition at its extravagant best, while the late Hubert Eaton, of Forest Lawn Memorial Park, could be taken as a symbol of the booster phase in its most ludicrous manifestations. Near neighbors in Los Angeles for many years, Aline Barnsdall ringed her beautiful Olive Hill estate, crowned with a fine Frank Lloyd Wright home, with flamboyant billboards urging freedom for Tom Mooney, while at no great distance, Aimee Semple McPherson, at Angeles Temple, staged evangelical shindigs for the entertainment of Iowa transplants. Job Harriman, the Socialist, was once nearly elected mayor of Los Angeles; today the office is held by Sam Yorty.

*   *   *

This volume is a collective attempt—a labor of love one might say—to tell the story of the California Revolution in the period since 1945: the advances and reversals, the achievements and setbacks, the fine creative efforts, and the mindless destruction. Today the California Revolution is entering a new phase. The population is growing, but with a difference (see the chapter by D. B. Luten). The former self-consciousness is still evident but a spirit of self-criticism is emerging. The rapid extension of certain trends has begun to meet with resistance, and counter trends have been set in motion. It is not surprising that the first all-auto state (see the chapter by Richard G. Lillard) should also be the state which should stage the first successful freeway revolt (see the chapter by Samuel E. Wood). Nor is it surprising, given some knowledge of the state's peculiar dynamics, that senseless inroads on the environment should have converted the old-style hiking, fishing, and mountain-climbing Sierra Club into a militant conservation organization—one of the toughest in the country (see the chapter by Scott Thurber). The state that has had so much to do with the development of the initiative, referendum, and recall has now begun to have second thoughts about these measures, once regarded as the indispensable tools of progressive government (see the chapter by Art Seidenbaum). The cults still thrive, but they are more sophisticated. The quest for the amenities is more evident than ever, but critics have begun to raise embarrassing questions (see the chapter by Robert Kirsch). At the moment, political reaction has triumphed in California but, predictably, the pendulum will soon swing in the other direction.

It would be a mistake to conclude that the California Revolution is slowing down or that its energies are dissipating. Californians are ingenious, resourceful, and inventive. If the state's war industries should suffer some cutbacks, the space program and other fields offer new and expanding opportunities to utilize the amazing pool of scientific and technological talent which the state has pirated and husbands so carefully (see the chapter by Wesley Marx). If the prospects for stealing more water from other regions are not as good as they once were, well, there is sea water and it can be desalinized. If the forward thrust has abated somehow, one may be fairly confident that there is more to come. The vast and mysterious world of the Pacific—"the chief theatre of the world in the world's great hereafter," as Seward called it— is stirring to a new life, and California is very much a part of that world, although Californians have seldom been aware of their relationship to it.

Out there, across the Pacific, is the island continent of Australia, with a land area about the size of this country and a population roughly comparable to that of New York City. Australia wants new settlers and capital; California has capital and population and is beginning to feel the need to export both. Australia has been handicapped (as California was at one time) by the myth that it is largely a desert, barren of resources. Nothing could be further from the truth. Take a look, for example, at mineral resources. "Seldom in history has there been anything like it," reports *Business Week* (August 7, 1965), "great globs of minerals, mountain after mountain of the richest iron ore in the world, cliffs of almost pure bauxite. . . . Australia is sitting on top of what appear to be the richest mineral finds of the century. Its great 'Outback' is suddenly up front, and the world is beating a path to its door." (See also "Mineral Boom in the 'Lucky Country' " by Harry Gordon, *The New York Times Magazine,* November 12, 1967; "Striking It Rich Down Under," *Business Week,* March 4, 1967; "Australia's Mineral Discoveries" by Nigel Calder, *New Scientist,* April 28, 1966.)

Most of these finds have been made subsequent to 1960: in oil, natural gas, bauxite, iron ore. Australia, it develops, is virtually the sole producer in the non-Communist world of rutile, a mineral sand of very great importance in the development of supersonic passenger planes because it makes possible titanium, the glistening, heat-resistant metal used in their production.

As one might expect, California companies are among those first in on what *The Wall Street Journal* calls "the new Australian boom" (January 20, 1968). Kaiser Steel Corporation, of Oakland, California, has a major stake in the new iron ore finds which are among "the world's purest" (*The Wall Street Journal,* December 23, 1966).

But the magnet of Australia consists of more than minerals. It has great agricultural possibilities. Cotton, of course, is a "migrating crop," and production is already beginning to shift from California's San Joaquin Valley to Australia (*Business Week,* August 5, 1967). A colony of 150 ex-Californians last year harvested 28,000 acres of cotton near Wee Waa in the Namoi River Valley of New South Wales. "A rush for riches," reports *U. S. News & World Report* (May 1, 1967), "bigger than any gold rush in history, now has gotten under way in Australia." Discount such statements as you will, there is truth in them.

Moreover, a combination of new factors is certain to further the Australia-California connection in the future. For one thing there has been—and will continue to be—a great increase in trans-Pacific air traffic, both of passengers and of air freight. In aviation there is a saying, "the longer the hop, the higher the profit." The trans-Pacific hop is a long one, but it is extremely profitable and the competition for it is already keen. Rates will drop as the passenger traffic increases (*Business Week,* February 11, 1967). The size of the planes will increase, with huge sky buses (for passengers) and big cargo planes (for freight).

American firms, sensing Australia's great future, are buying in; there were some 1,700 of them in 1967 and they owned about 8 per cent of all Australian company assets (*Congressional Record,* August 30, 1967, p. S. 12600). As Britain has been forced to cut its investments, American capital, a lot of it from California, has moved in. The British military withdrawal from the Far East, which will be completed by 1971, has forced Australia to strengthen its American ties. The change is symbolized by its shift from pounds, shillings, and pence to dollars and cents, as monetary units.

But the reverse is also true: Walter Lippmann has been merely one of a number of publicists who have advocated a "Fortress Australia" policy for America in the Far East. We need Australia just as Australia needs us. Already the trade around the rim of the Pacific is expanding rapidly; it has grown at about 10 per cent per annum since 1955, making it one of the most interesting areas of international commerce. And the trade which has developed is only a small part of what it will be in time. At the moment, the California-Australia phase of this trade is still in its infancy.

The headlines tell the story of what is to come: "The American 'Invasion' of Australia," announces *Newsweek,* August 10, 1964, is now under way, "with a rising investment tide which surpasses $1.2 billion." It is this prospect, which has hardly yet been sensed by the Californians, that holds such bright continuing promise for the future of the state. Already the trans-Pacific migration has begun; it will certainly increase.

These developments make R. T. Appleyard's contribution to this volume of special interest and a proper note on which to bring it to a close. No, the California Revolution is not over by any means; there are many more chapters to come. Some will be brilliant, some dismaying, all of them exciting. No one, including John Morgan, knows what California will be like in the year 2000, but one thing is clear: California is the future.

D. B. Luten

THE DYNAMICS
OF REPULSION

Edmund G. Brown, when he was governor, would speak with enthusiasm in election years of the growth of California. In the alternate (budget) years, he spoke with concern of the numbers problem. Late in the evening of November 8, 1966, when he conceded the election to Ronald Reagan, his own feelings were not in evidence. But Mrs. Brown stood by his side with an undisguised grin on her face. One wonders if she was thinking about 1967, a budget year. One also wonders how other Americans, the one-tenth who are Californians and the nine-tenths who are not, should look at the problems of California and its growth.

Everyone knows that California is growing, and it is common to think of this as a recent phenomenon. Thus, the increase of 3.5 million (from 15.7 million in April, 1960, to 19.2 million in July, 1966) is greater than that witnessed in any other six-year period for California or any other state. Again, between 1940 and 1950, the population grew by 5 million—surely a state record for a decade and as sure to be broken in 1970.

However, there is another way to look at population growth, a way we use all the time in other contexts. This is to measure the annual increase as a percentage of the existing population. For comparisons, it seems more rational. For instance, you will jeer at me if I say, "Imagine, the Rockefellers made a million dollars from their investments last year!" But you will be impressed if I say, "J. Doe made a million last year on a capital of ten thousand dollars." So, also, an increase in Wyoming's population by 5 million would be more startling (and more traumatic) than the California growth.

It may be objected that California's growth is not all internally generated; the major part of it has always been by immigration, some from foreign countries, most from other states. Thus, while growth before 1849 was internally generated and small, with the Gold Rush it became enormous. Putting aside qualms on this score, how has the state grown?

The record is unexpected: viewed broadly, the growth rate of California's population has been constant for a century. While it has grown more rapidly in one decade than another, ranging from least (2 per cent) in the Depression to greatest (5.2 per cent) in the 1920s, if one looks at the entire interval from 1860 to 1960, the tale is simple: the population, on the average, has grown at 3.8 per cent per year, doubling each 18.5 years, over the century. The increase totals more than fortyfold. The slow decades and the fast decades were so closely associated that the overall trend is one of spectacular regularity. The 1890s were slow but were followed by the prosperous 1900s and the deficit in numbers was made up. The Depression was a period of low birth rates and, contrary to popular belief, also of low immigration. But it was preceded by the 1920s, with heavy immigration, so that by 1930 the population was "ahead of the curve." Then followed the war decade which made up the deficit, so that by 1950 the state was back on the curve. And it stayed there in 1960.

Natural increase has ranged eightfold from a low of approximately 0.3 per cent per year for the Depression decade to a high of about 2 per cent in the 1870s. The general trend has been one of slow decline, with a sharp drop in the 1930s, followed by a postwar upsurge almost to the level of a century ago. During most of these hundred years, Warren Thompson has calculated, families were too small to have maintained a constant population had immigration ceased.

Immigration, surprisingly, has varied less, ranging from a low of a little over 1 per cent per year in the 1890s to a high of more than 4 per cent in the 1920s. It has always carried the burden of growth, providing from 55 per cent (1870s) to 85 per cent (1930s).

When one looks at the state regionally, similar irregularities appear. In 1860, a third of all Californians lived in the San Francisco Bay Area and another third in the Sierra foothill gold country. Less than 5 per cent were in the south coastal region. Today, the Bay Area has shrunk to a fifth, the mountain counties to less than 5 per cent, while the south coast has grown to half.

So much for the past. Today, many of the trends persist. First, California's birth rate remains lower, but only a shade lower, than the nation's, and it has declined, as has the nation's, from a postwar peak in 1957. From this high of almost 25 infants annually per 1,000 persons in California, and just over 25 for the nation, the rate dropped in 1964 to 20.6 for California and 21.7 for the United States. Whether it will rise again within the next few years, when the postwar babies marry, is still uncertain. Californians will probably continue to have slightly smaller families than Americans as a whole.

Second, distribution of growth within the state continues to deviate widely from the average. Between 1960 and 1965, Orange County on the fringe of Los Angeles grew at 10 per cent per year, while five other counties had a very slight population loss. Four of these counties, in the northern Sierra Nevada, were small. The fifth is San Francisco, city and county, so urban that increasing metropolitan functions leave less and less room for living. Los Angeles County grows at about the rate for the entire state; the San Francisco Bay Area grows more slowly. Suburban counties grow more rapidly. All of these trends are plausible.

Although doubts may be voiced as to the urbanity of California's cities, statistically it is the least rural of the states. Close to 90 per cent of its residents are classed as urban. Among the many causes which could be cited the most obvious is the mechanization and low man power requirement of its extractive industries. Do not, though, overlook the effect on the great cities of national publicity. With immigration providing the bulk of growth and immigrants educated by press and TV, growth gravitates to massive centers. Everyone in New York has heard of Los Angeles, but how many know of Placerville?

Third, age distribution in California is not as usually imagined: compared to the United States as a whole, California is a little deficient in elderly folk and has a small surplus of young adults.

Fourth, it is commonly thought that migrants become more and more the disadvantaged, the deprived, the poor, who escape from a bad into what they hope will be a better environment. Whether this is so I cannot say. At one time it appeared that immigrants from the Southwest came to the agricultural land of the Central Valley, were only transiently employed, and had to return to the family farm for the winter. They commonly made the seasonal migration for summer farm work several times before developing a niche of stable employment in California. How many times might such an immgirant be counted? In contrast, immigrants from the Northeast were believed to be going to California's cities, already assured of jobs or confident of employment. For example, within a stone's throw of my home, three new families arrived from out of state within a year. But all of these were corporate transfers, and were replacing equal numbers of emigrants. How shall we count these migrants?

In fact, one must hedge today on the patterns of immigration. Assessment of immigrants by automobile has been undertaken, but did the poorest arrive by car? Was the state of previous registration the state of origin, or did the person or family reach California only after several stops along the way? Disregarding these substantial doubts, immigrants today seem to obey reasonable laws of diffusion; more from populous areas, fewer from remote areas. Net annual immigration per 100,000 persons in the area of origin amounts to about 200 for the eleven Western states, around 500 for the plains, 550 for the Southwest, 150 for the Southeast, 300 for the North Central, and 200 for the Northeastern states.

One pattern that emerges clearly is that the slightly younger California population is being made still younger by immigrants. Those entering the state are rarely elderly. The proportion of persons over forty years of age is lower than in the state's population. The fraction of immigrants between twenty and thirty is almost twice the fraction of residents of the state in that age group. Children under five are also more frequent among immigrants than among residents, but older children, plausibly, are scarcer. The picture, then, is one of immigration of young adults with young children.

In recent years, approximately 60 per cent of the state's growth has been due to immigration, 40 per cent to natural increase. This comes to 1,000 per day net migration, the difference between 2,000 immigrants and 1,000 emigrants. These numbers reflect the high mobility of the American population, the loss among many of them of traditional attitudes about where to live. Americans will go where they are attracted, will leave places which repel them.

At present, however, a decrease is occurring, as shown in the tabulation below.

But one year does not make a decade, much less a century. What comes next? Early in 1966, a brief press flurry arose when the State Department of Finance, the reputable and competent source of most of my data, released a statement that immigration to the state had ceased. Stopped dead. The test, a neat one, was that the population of school children in the third to the eighth grades was no greater than the population the year before of children in the second to seventh grades. The test is good because no children are born into this group, very few die out of it, very few drop out of school; the only change is due to migration. It assumes only that family patterns do not change rapidly, an assumption justified by experience. A week later the statement was retracted and it was explained that a change had taken place in the manner of assembling the data and that some reports had stuck in the new channels and had been overlooked. Immigration has not, in fact, ceased.

Enough of the present. What of the future? First, note that California cannot continue to grow forever, or even for a very long period, at a greater rate than the nation. Simple arithmetic shows that if California maintains its growth rate at the traditional 3.8 per cent per year and the nation maintains its rate at the 1.6 per cent of 1960, then in about 110 years, say 2070, the populations of both the United States and California would be about a billion. That is, all Americans would live in California. This seems unlikely.

Year (July 1)	Population (millions)	Natural Increase (thousands)	Net Immigration (thousands)
1958	14.7	226	325
1961	16.5	224	346
1964	18.2	230	352
1967	19.5	187	250

Growth Rate, per cent per year		
Calif.	U. S.	Calif. minus U. S.
4.0	1.7	2.3
3.7	1.7	2.0
3.1	1.4	1.7
2.1	1.0	1.1

No one expects such a result. Continuance at 3.8 per cent per year leads to 72 million Californians in the year 2000, 100 million in 2020. But estimates have rarely been for more than 45 million in 2000 and no one cares to project to 2020. Recent projections suggest less growth by century's end, and the State Department of Finance's current projection is for 39 to 42 million.

If there are not to be 72 million Californians at the end of the century, then California's growth rate must diminish. What will cause this to occur? The answer can be given in the form of a truism, and it must be emphasized that this answer is only a truism. It was phrased a few years ago in these terms:

California will stop growing one day because it will have become just as repulsive as the rest of the country.

The phrasing is provocative because of the twofold implications of "repulsive" meaning simply to repel like a magnetic field, but also carrying the sense of "disgusting," "repugnant," "distasteful." Taken at its face value, it says Americans will go where they are attracted, will leave where they are repelled. Today, they are more attracted than repelled by California; the day must come when as many are repelled as attracted.

Chemistry has an analogous term, the "fugacity," the escaping tendency, the tendency to flee. A gas tends to flee from a region of high fugacity to a region of lower fugacity and, as a result, its escaping tendency approaches equality in the two places. All people have tended to escape unhappy environments, to seek better ones. This is one of the essences of humanity. What else is hope? In the past its expression was slow; migration reflected bitter unrest. Today, it is easier.

The analogy suggests only that migration will continue until the escaping tendency is equal everywhere; until, on the average, for each easterner who sees greener pastures in the West, a westerner will see them in the East. How fast the adjustment will occur, how fast reaction to a vision of withering pastures will take place, is another matter. Willingness to migrate has been increasing for centuries, but even in the nineteenth century, migration was not for the timid, the secure, the provident, the affluent; rather it was for the bold, the disinherited, the wastrel, the indigent. Provincialism, ignorance of remote lands, myths of perils along the way, all of these limited equilibration. Today, most Americans see California daily on the TV screen, know that its customs, its hostelries for the itinerant differ but little from those of Maine or South Carolina, and they have a pretty clear notion of job opportunities in Los Angeles and San Jose. "If you think California is the promised land, fly out this weekend and have a look. But be back for work Monday!" Or case the entire state next vacation.

By and large, it is inescapable that equilibration is more rapid today than yesterday. If the fugacity relative to the rest of the country has not changed, then migration should have increased. Since it has not, the attractive force of California must be dropping.

A reasonable corollary of this combination of increasing mobility and decreasing difference in escaping tendency is that migration will not dwindle slowly, in a "normal" fashion, but rather will drop quite precipitately, "abnormally."

This does not mean that every American is on the move. What concerns us is marginal mobility. Correspondingly, if California becomes repulsive, not all residents will be repelled. Some are immune to smog, many are protected against most aspects of repulsiveness. But the quite few marginally mobile people reflect and influence social and economic conditions and cannot, therefore, be ignored.

If growth will end with nationally uniform repulsiveness (and attractiveness), what is the anatomy of repulsiveness and attractiveness? A host of visions comes to mind. On the one hand: roses and sunshine in December, cool fog in summer, picnicking without rain, sunny beaches, magnificent mountains, coast lines, forests, vast empty lands, all near at hand; action, the metropolis of glamour always in the very pupil of the public eye; the metropolis of beauty, ringed by sea, hills, and bay; great universities. But on the other: crowded, stinking, smarting air, crowded highways, whether at weekend's close or workday's end; crowded schools, crowded prisons, crowded sewers; exorbitant taxes, instability, cranks and extremism from wing to wing; dissension, incipient revolution, unrest, unrest, unrest! Did everyone who went to California go because he couldn't get along with his neighbors?

Visions and knowledge of nearer places also swing the balance. What makes the climate of the Northeast repulsive? Those mid-week winter storms, when you must shovel the driveway and hit the road in the gloom! Our grandparents stayed in and read "Snowbound"; we must go to work. Where have the water shortages been close to home? In the East.

At the base of all of this must lie jobs. A man does have to make a living. Where are the jobs? Are the space age contractors hiring? Fifteen thousand new openings at Lockheed, in Sunnyvale on the San Francisco peninsula, mean 15,000 new employees, 30,000 new dependents, and perhaps another 25,000 workers, and their 50,000 dependents, to supply and distribute goods and services to the entire 120,000.

The greatest determinant of immigration must be the assurance, the realistic prospect or the vision of employment. Unemployment is higher in California than nationally. One of Governor Reagan's first campaign promises was that he would do better at creating new jobs than had Governor Brown. But, transparently, if he does create new jobs, resident Californians will not have a prior right to them. New jobs will create new immigrants. The only thing proved by high unemployment in California is that the state is still more attractive, less repulsive, than the rest of the country. The mobile American will still take a greater chance on being unemployed in California than elsewhere. This, too, will change.

Three years ago, a conference entitled "Man in California, 1980's" spent two days on the almost insuperable problems facing California in the next two decades: polluted air with the prospect of $2 billion a year to be spent merely to maintain the present distressing status, polluted water, growing imbalance in water supply; agriculture disappearing under suburbs, deteriorating urban transport and an unremitting struggle to improve highway transport; overcrowded parks, littered beaches, vanishing wildlife; urban slums, a perennial focus of unemployment; increasing crime, disturbed minds. All of these typical American phenomena, the discussion made quite clear, were to be most severe in California because of California's unremitting growth. The last act of the conference was to present a most convincing outline of the enormous task involved in attracting new industry to California, burdened by high taxes, long hauls, restrictive legislation. And yet, by virtue of the extraordinary competence of those searching for new industry, complete success on this score was to be expected. So here we have it: entire agreement that the state's problems are associated with its growth, and yet growth must be maintained. Do we conclude that a fate worse than an environment in ruins is an economy in ruins?

Growth means new jobs and new jobs mean growth. On this merry-go-round, which is cart and which is horse? And what drives the merry-go-round?

It must be suspected that claims on the national economy drive the state's economy. If California can buy from the nation what it wants, first with gold, then wheat, then citrus fruits, then retirements, then oil, then movies, tourism, and entertainment, California can grow. But the gold is gone; the wheat has given way to barley to feed livestock consumed in California; Florida and Texas competition is rough on citrus; the subdivisions creep over the Class I crop land; Florida and Arizona have the retirement market; the oil is dwindling, natural gas is imported from Texas and

Alberta; movies are made elsewhere; Californians spend as much outside California on vacation as outsiders spend in California; only a small portion of entertainment receipts is spent in California. What, then, is left?

Three items: First, cash receipts from agriculture are still great. Second, more of California's industrial needs are being provided locally; California needs less per capita from outside. Third, California's immigrants bring credit from the East and an insatiable appetite to consume. California has sold its resources, now it is selling its future.

"Foster City—Lagoon Living, 3 bedrooms de luxe, $31,750, $233.27 per month, taxes and insurance included, for 35 years." To the end of the century.

"How much is this mountain side (with a narrow overlook of Lake Tahoe)?" "$700 an acre." "But last year that Saxon Creek land sold for $350." "$350 last year, $700 this year; isn't that about right?"

As long as the immigration continues, California can continue on the merry-go-round, can continue to live in the land of the Red Queen. But the Red Queen is debt, and she is in splendid running condition. How long will the race last?

The answer is easy. So long as eastern creditors believe California's growth will continue. If a state has a housing industry growing at the interest rate (say, 3.8 per cent per year) and financed from outside, then for the first amortization cycle of twenty-five years the region receives more credit, can buy more from outsiders, than it has to return in monthly payments. After a full cycle of payments, each month's payments just provide the credit for next month's new starts. But when growth slackens, the monthly payments will be more than the credit advanced for the current starts. And when the growth stops, credit for new houses becomes zero, but the payments will continue for another twenty-five years. The assumptions that the housing industry grows at the interest rate and is financed from outside are not quite true, but each of them is close enough to outline an ominous picture. When the growth stops, what will California do to pay its way, to buy what it needs from the other states, in addition to paying off its mortgage holders in those states? And if householders come to be without jobs, will foreclosure help creditors? Will the householders already have emigrated or, still in occupancy, will they offer to protect the house from the neighborhood kids if the title holder pays a nominal watchman's fee?

The forecasts of California's growth are self-fulfilling forecasts. As long as they are believed, growth will continue. When they become incredible, growth will end. The mistaken announcement last February that growth had ceased was a remarkable act of bureaucratic integrity. If the statisticians had, in fact, decided that growth was about to end, would growth have ended?

Look now at the record of housing starts, of savings and loans failures, of residential vacancies. In spite of this record, which is disturbing, if we may judge from the level of unemployment, which remains high, California is not yet repulsive.

Finally, it has also been said that when growth ends in California, the party out of power will be congratulating itself for a decade. So the final questions remain. What *was* Governor Brown thinking of when, after that dead political campaign, he conceded the election to Ronald Reagan? And how can California remain attractive without attracting its ruin?

Mel Wax

THE KNOWLEDGE BONANZA

Outside California, the state's seventy-eight junior colleges and eighteen state colleges make, perhaps, less of an academic, social, and psychedelic splash than do the nine campuses and 87,000 students of the University of California. But within the state's tripartite system of higher education, established under the 1960 Master Plan for Higher Education, they loom very large indeed— and larger every year.

Right now, for example, nearly 600,000 full- and part-time students, ranging from overblown teenie-boppers to overaged grandmas, are enrolled in two-year junior colleges, and the number grows by more than 10 per cent a year. And 172,000 students in the four-year state colleges are studying everything from aeronautics to zoology. Some are heading for master's degrees; others for doctorates.

There is nothing like this, anywhere else in the world. If you're fortunate enough to be a Californian, you can now advance from kindergarten to doctor of philosophy in tuition-free public schools that are said to compare in quality with the best anywhere in the Western world. In quantity, there is no comparison at all.

But less than one week after Ronald Reagan was sworn in as governor, he was hanged in effigy by the students of Fresno State College. He had recommended a 10 per cent cut in higher education budgets, and had added the suggestion that it might be a good idea for university and state college students to pay tuition. Students, educators, politicians, and even such stalwarts of conservatism as Republican regent Dorothy Buffum Chandler, of the powerful Los Angeles *Times* dynasty, were furious.

While California's sun-kissed students are charged no tuition, they do pay relatively modest "fees," and in junior colleges they also pay up to $10 a year for health services and parking privileges—the *sine qua non* of California life. In state colleges, annual fees range from $96 to $102, at the university—depending on the campus—they might be as much as $243 a year.

Louis H. Heilbron, state college trustee and former chairman of the State Board of Education, justifies the system:

> Educators believe that, in the long run, California will suffer rather than benefit from any kind of tuition charge. The dollars spent on higher education usually come back multiplied in the form of increased tax contributions to the local federal and state governments after the student leaves the college or university campus.

While junior colleges are supported, for the most part, by local communities, state colleges operate on state funds, as does the University of California. For the eighteen state college campuses (four more will open soon), Chancellor Glenn S. Dumke asked $252.8 million in fiscal 1967–68. New state colleges, each of them expected to zoom to an enrollment of 20,000 students soon after their parking lots open and their pom-pom girls are chosen, cost $120 million apiece, about the price of a nuclear submarine.

Four of five California high school graduates live within commuting distance of a junior college. All they need to enroll is a high school diploma, and if they are eighteen years old, they don't need even that. For the high school dropout, or the late educational bloomer, junior colleges offer salvation. Under the Master Plan, the university accepts the top 12.5 per cent of high school graduates in California; state colleges, the top 33⅓ per cent, and junior colleges take the rest.

Many junior college students later transfer to state colleges, and some make it to the University of California. During the first semester, transferees to the university score from .1 to .2 points lower than their new colleagues. Thereafter, academic performance is the same. This probably says a lot for the motivation of the students accepted by the university, and for the quality of junior college teachers.

The quality, personality, and goals of state colleges vary. Some are strong in agriculture, others are urban-oriented. Some specialize in engineering and science, others in the arts and humanities. All told, they produce three-fourths of California's elementary and secondary school teachers. But they are not mass educational factories, as some of their critics insist.

At San Francisco State College, for example, students run their own Experimental College. They have a staff of eighty-five students and forty faculty. Paul Goodman, the noted critic of stereotyped education, was a visiting professor last year. Under this plan, more than 1,200 of San Francisco State's 18,400 students have participated in seminars ranging from "Cybernetics and LSD: A Study of the Application of Consciousness-Expanding Drugs to Technology," to "Revolutionary Capitalism" and "Conscientious Objection." And balancing these esoteric topics, seminars have dealt with such conventional subject matter as "Soviet Civilization" and "Human Growth and Development."

"I've been through the panty-raid period of student activity," said San Francisco State College President John Summerskill, commenting on the experimental college, "and visited campuses where the rah-rah spirit prevails, or where students are making direct attacks on authority as such.

"Here we have hundreds of students concerned with education, and I can't think of a better thing for them to be concerned about. The main business of the college is learning; that's what the taxpayers provide our salaries and buildings for."

Growth of the state colleges and junior colleges boomed in California following World War II. It thus parallels the state's spectacular population explosion, but, while the overall population of California is increasing by 38 per cent between 1960 and 1970, the college-age population will grow by 90 per cent. And the end is not in sight.

In 1921, there were seven teachers' colleges in the state, and this count remained steady until 1935, when they were officially designated "State Colleges." California State College at Los Angeles had 147 students when it opened in 1947, in skimpy, borrowed quarters on the Los Angeles City College campus. Ten years later it had moved to a lavish 97-acre spread and attracted 8,383 students. Today it has an enrollment of 20,000. California State College at Long Beach began in a rented apartment building in 1949, with a handful of students. It moved to permanent facilities in 1954. Eleven years later it had an enrollment of 20,845. A new state college—they stretch from Humboldt State near the Oregon border to San Diego State on the Mexican border—is built every other year. From 1935 to 1953, enrollment in state colleges jumped from 8,230 to 41,000 full-time students. Four years later, it had doubled. Today's total of 172,000 is expected to reach 225,000 by the end of the decade, and Chancellor Dumke predicts that in 1981 there will be 300,000 students on twenty-five campuses at a budget of $500 million.

California junior colleges date from 1907, when an enlightened state legislature told high schools they could expand to include the first two years of college. None took advantage of this opportunity until Fresno City College was created in 1910, the second oldest American public junior college in continuous operation. (The oldest is Joliet Junior College, in Illinois.) The next year, Santa Barbara High School became a junior college and, by the time the United States was fighting in World War I, there were sixteen, with a total enrollment of 1,259.

After World War II, when everything big in California exploded into something bigger, junior colleges tried to become four-year colleges, and state colleges, universities. The pressures on the legislature were tremendous. In 1959, for instance, twenty-three bills were introduced on behalf of various communities wanting their own college or university. Higher education has become the status symbol for the insecure Westerner, proof that each mountain town or desert hamlet has achieved culture, or at least knows some place close by where it can be had for the asking.

The legislators then decided it was time to call a halt to the uncontrolled, unplanned mushrooming of higher education—no matter how offensive such a check might seem to ebullient Californians and to their faith in an unlimited horizon. A commission of eight top California educators, headed by Dr. Arthur G. Coons, president of Occidental College, was told to bring order out of the jealousies and internecine warfare that threatened to split the strata of California's education mountain.

In 1960, the commission drew up a plan that nobody completely endorsed. It called for separating state colleges from the State Board of Education, and giving them their own Board of State College Trustees, modeled on the university's Board of Regents. Junior colleges would remain with the State Board of Education.

Some thought state colleges should stay where they were; others favored a super board of education to ride herd on state colleges, junior colleges, and the university. Finally, Governor Edmund G.

Brown called warring factions to his office and told them they had labored too hard and too long for a Master Plan to lose it in the end. "Let's make it the law." They did, by unanimous legislative endorsement. Looking back recently on his eight years as governor, Brown called it his proudest achievement.

The Master Plan decreed that the University of California should be empowered to teach all subjects, and be the primary research institution. It would be the source of doctorates, but a state college, in collaboration with a university campus, could work out a "joint doctorate" program.

The university was to have sole jurisdiction over education in law, medicine, veterinary medicine, dentistry, and graduate courses in architecture. This, it was hoped would concentrate teaching talent, and occasion a minimum duplication of expensive equipment.

State colleges were given jurisdiction in the liberal arts and sciences, plus such professions as teaching, engineering, social work, and other disciplines, up to and including the master's degree, that had not been staked out for the University of California.

Junior colleges, under the plan, could offer two-year Associate in Arts degrees, and were given exclusive rights to terminal vocational education. They were also entrusted with the task of providing two years of general education at the college level for students planning to transfer to state colleges or to the university.

It was proposed that by 1975, 50,000 undergraduates who otherwise would enter state colleges or the university would be diverted to junior colleges for their freshman and sophomore years. Sixty per cent of the enrollment at state colleges and the university would then be upperclassmen. In 1965, for the first time, more than half the new state college students came from junior colleges. The ratio was lower at the university.

The Master Plan called on the state of California to pay 45 per cent of the annual operating costs of the junior colleges by 1975, freeing them to that degree from dependence on local property taxes. (The state, through a series of bond issues, has since helped junior colleges substantially with plant-expansion programs.)

The Master Plan for Higher Education in California has served as a model not only for other states but also for other nations. Great Britain sent a delegation to study it when the English were planning for expansion; so did France.

How well has the Master Plan worked? Better than expected, but not so well as it could. The statistics on California's knowledge bonanza are impressive, but the ultimate measure must be whether or not the educational program achieves the goals assigned to it.

In 1967, for the first time, junior colleges decreed that a "C" average would be required for graduation. As Thomas W. Braden, former president of the Board of Education, carefully explained, that doesn't mean a "get tough" policy for junior college students. Anybody failing to achieve a "C" average for three consecutive semesters is subject to dismissal, but he can be readmitted. "The junior college," said Paul Lawrence, head of the State Department of Education's Division of Higher Learning, "is a place of opportunity, so he can come back again and again."

But in Braden's view junior colleges are not fulfilling their role. "The weakness of the system is that, as it has grown in California, it has tended to neglect its role as a terminal institution for vocational preparation," Braden said. "It has done so for two reasons: First, the vocational role is expensive; second, it is unprestigious."

Braden, an Oceanside newspaper publisher, suggested that the state might set up a new and separate set of vocational colleges, supported by state rather than local funds. He made the same proposal to Governor Brown some time ago. It received passing notice in a campaign speech, but nothing has been heard of it since.

Prestige is a disease that afflicts state colleges as well as junior colleges. It is significant that almost every one of the seventy-eight junior colleges in California has dropped the offending word "junior" from its title. They are trying to build faculties of Ph.D.'s, not auto mechanics. The state college system, with a faculty of some 10,000, also has recruiting problems. California must lure most of its college teachers from outside the state, and pay higher than average salaries. However, the professional status, the big federal research grants, the easier teaching loads go with university appointments, not with state college jobs.

Marc R. Tool, a professor of economics at Sacramento State College, was commissioned recently by the Academic Senate of the State College System to study the effect of the Master Plan upon these colleges. He has found, in a 200-page report, that they are "victims" of academic discrimination:

> The Master Plan, by design and by interpretation, has become a vehicle through which the California State Colleges have been relegated to an inferior and subordinate position relative to the University of California.
>
> Given the directive that each segment shall strive for excellence, the Master Plan has created a condition in which the State colleges cannot aspire to excellence because they are not provided with adequate financial means and the relevant policy options to make possible the achievement of excellence of which they are capable.

According to Professor Tool, the university gets 58 per cent of state support funds for 38 per cent of the students, while state colleges limp along with 42 per cent of the money for 62 per cent of the students. He contends that the university professor gets more pay, more sabbaticals, more secretarial and technical help, more research money, and a lighter teaching load than his state college counterpart.

Junior colleges make similar complaints. The Arthur D. Little Company, a private research firm, recently recommended that they be divorced from the State Board of Education and given their own chancellor, and their own bureaucracy, as are state colleges and the university.

Junior college faculty members consider themselves oppressed. A teacher at College of Marin, just north of San Francisco, complained that when he gave his students failing grades in English he was rebuked by his superiors on the ground that either his course was too difficult or he was grading too hard. The possibility that his students were not bright enough was not considered.

"If what they want is some kind of social welfare program to keep kids off the streets for two years after high school, O.K.," added his wife. "But let's be honest about it. Let's not call it a college. And let's use social workers for teachers."

The junior colleges, like state colleges, observe varying standards of excellence, and they have different objectives. Some offer strong academic courses in general education, and are successful in producing transfer students for state colleges and the university. Others concentrate on terminal education, and still others on vocational training.

At one time, the ratio of academic and vocational programs in California junior colleges was half and half. Now the pendulum has swung heavily to the academic side. The new trend is typified by Foothill College, which has an extensive liberal arts curriculum. Less than ten years old, this campus in the foothills of the Santa Cruz Mountains of Northern California has more than 7,000 students on its magnificent 122 acres.

Foothill's thirty-six brick and redwood buildings, including an Olympic-sized swimming pool and a one-acre library, and its sheltered, car-free pedestrian walks, give it an atmosphere of quiet, rural peace and isolation. Within a 1,000-seat auditorium, blessed with near-perfect acoustics, students learn the performing arts by performing them, and both students and nearby Los Altos residents enjoy guest performances of the San Francisco Symphony and other traveling artists. One of the great benefits of the state and junior college system in California is the intellectual and cultural impact of the colleges on communities where they are located.

Foothill also has a 3,500-car parking lot, the essential ingredient for a community college that depends on commuters. There are no dormitories at Foothill, nor are there any at most junior colleges, or at many state colleges. Foothill puts heavy emphasis on liberal arts. But it also offers Associate in Arts degrees in data processing, electronics, industrial ceramics, and other arcane specialities. Graduates frequently are snapped up at starting salaries of $900 a month.

Whatever its faults and problems, California characteristically and vigorously has launched a massive program of democratic higher education on a scale never before attempted by any state or nation. That there are shortcomings is not surprising. What is remarkable is the abounding optimism, the monumental scope, and the high promise of the effort.

Wesley Marx

ONE-EYED
TECHNOLOGY

As the aerospace technocracy accomplishes space-spectaculars launch after televised launch, a question keeps insisting itself. If space engineers can get men into orbit, why can't they help get us to work faster? Other dreamlike variations include: If space scientists can make instruments germ-free in space, why can't they help retard the pollution of our air and water? If engineers can transmit photographs through millions of miles of space, why can't they transmit enough information to keep track of our criminals?

A sense of dismay lurks behind the simplistic "application" question. Our technological brainpower, nurtured by multimillion-dollar-bond adventures in higher education, gravitates into one area, the aerospace industry. Success in this industry seems to come in direct proportion to the distance from earth. Races are the vogue: the missile race, the space race, now the inner space

36

(ocean) race. Where is the smog race? Is advanced technology really a new form of escape fiction, the soul mate of a narcissistic national security that demands more power and more prestige?

The Application Question has special significance in one state. Postwar California is, to a great degree, a creature of the national security economy. An amalgam of defense and space contracts supports an extensive aerospace establishment, and this establishment dominates the state's activities in manufacturing, employment, and university research. At chamber of commerce luncheons or state tax hearings, aerospace presidents fondly declare "that aerospace and related defense activities account for one of every ten civilian jobs, four of every ten manufacturing jobs, a third of all industrial output, and from a third to a half of total personal income in Southern California." (Applause) With its classified think factories, its rocket factories, and its supersonics factories, the aerospace community imbues California with glamour as well as growth. Industry recruiters, known affectionately as brain pirates, assiduously recruit prestige immigrants, such as electronics engineers, physicists, and retired Navy admirals. ("Work with the Future—Contact John Martin Collect.")

Yet it is no coincidence that traffic congestion, air pollution, and crime reach seemingly insurmountable proportions in California. Besides helping to nurture such fast-tract growth, the burgeoning national security economy escalates automation to new heights. A "change in procurement" can lay off 5,000, 10,000, even 15,000 technical servants instantly. A drop in the defense budget threatens to lay off the whole industry. In California, it is not war that is hell.

In this insecure environment, congressmen regress into defense politicians, wailing the disarmament blues, charging that foreign congressmen are hi-jacking California contracts, forever pushing the high ground higher and reducing technology to mere defense contracts.

If the Application Question could be resolved in the affirmative, California could kill—or at least wing—two vultures with one stone: economic insecurity and environmental deterioration. Thus California finds itself forced to discover if the learned people who can put technology into orbit can bring it down to earth.

In 1962, Douglas's Skybolt missile contract was canceled. The number of people laid off—5,000—was not unusually large. But the men learned of their fate during the holiday season, thus dramatizing California's helpless and harsh aerospace dependency. The then governor, Edmund Brown, asked electronics and aerospace executives to meet regularly to discuss "the possibilities of conversion in the event of a continuing drop in space and defense contracts." That the aircraft industry, following World War II, failed to crack the voracious consumer economy with precision aluminum canoes and steel caskets stimulated new thinking. Recalls Brown, "When we began thinking in the terms of the public sector—of the many unmet needs of the community—we began to realize we have a precious and unused resource." This resource consists of systems engineers, "men who [have] been trained to think in totally new dimensions, to solve problems and create systems for carrying out missions unique in history." This concentration on the industry's managerial capability, rather than just its exotic products, reflects a common concern of many public policy makers. Urban problems—such as pollution—seem to be intensified by a welter of "home rule" fiefs that frustrate problem-oriented management and area-wide planning, the crux of systems management.

In 1964, in a demonstration run, California called for bids from aerospace firms to study and recommend programs in crime prevention, waste management, transportation, and government information systems. The four study contracts were funded at a modest $100,000 each.

Willard Wilks of *Aerospace Technology* (formerly *Missiles and Rockets*) asked one aerospace executive to size up this new aerospace "market." "You aren't going to get a Titan or Minuteman program out of it," was the reply. Despite this attitude, over fifty bids were received, a turnout any defense procurement official would envy.

The four winning bidders mobilized the inter-discipline teams that characterize systems management—economists, life scientists, computer specialists. These teams, in turn, began focusing the system techniques so common to the Pentagon—linear programming, cost-effectiveness analysis, decision theory, mathematical modeling, computer simulation—on sewage outfalls and traffic tie-ups. "At last I could talk about the work at the office to my wife at dinner," commented one scientist, normally restricted to classified work in the universe.

The studies were completed in late 1965. In the case of waste management, Aerojet-General viewed all facets of waste disposal—from sewer discharges to trash cans to auto exhausts—as a total system. The resulting view was almost comic. "Waste disposal" is transforming the waste of one person or one machine into a problem for another person. "Eye irritation caused by air pollution is a common complaint in the Los Angeles area. Many farms in the Central Valley (California's food basket) can now grow only salt-resistant plants because of inadequate drainage of irrigated land. . . . South San Francisco Bay has become offensive to sight and smell through its use as a cesspool." Sewage outfalls are even becoming the new monsters of the sea. "South coastal kelp beds (a commercially-harvested seaweed) have almost disappeared because of increased sewage emission to the ocean."

Waste non-management rests on a solid political footing. "There are many separate state and local bodies regulating, collecting and disposing of different wastes. No single organization is charged with managing all aspects to obtain a waste management system that will produce the desired effect at minimum cost."

People without the benefit of $100,000 contracts and computer time have been saying the same thing since the first outfall, the pipe, was invented; the real value of systems management emerges in showing how age-old problems can be resolved on a sound, scientific basis. Continued the Aerojet-General report, "Because of the ease of transforming many types of waste from one aggregate form into another, the waste management system should be one system, with gaseous, liquid, solid and radiological waste subsystems." Such a system would be established, not on the basis of the county line, but on economic and technical criteria— topographical and meteorological conditions, population density, land usage, and transportation patterns. Such a system could readily implement technical innovations—perhaps homesite grinders which would grind solid wastes fine enough for the sewer system and thus outmode the trash can collection. (The other side of this shiny coin, of course, is that garbage operators, like aerospace assemblers, would suddenly be exposed to the primitive job economics of technocracy.)

Using the tool of cost effectiveness, the study found that such an expansive system would actually be cheaper than the present system. Projecting into 1990, the study reported that the existing network of systems in California would cost $1.1 billion annually to operate and yet trigger pollution damages of $7.4 billion. An integrated and much-upgraded system would cost twice as much to operate, but, by deterring pollution, the overall cost would come to $3.7 billion. Concluded Aerojet-General, "High-quality environmental air, water and land can be obtained at expenditure levels far less than the social costs associated with a low-quality or 'least acceptable' environment."

The prospect of better service for lower cost the systems analysis way was reiterated in other study reports. A study by Lockheed concluded that an integrated and computerized Statewide Information System could save $170 million annually in waging the great paper war of government. A study by North American found that transportation technology to relieve urban congestion existed but that the economics of this technology required a broad-based systems approach. The Space-General study into crime prevention shows how a systems approach can cut through hoary slogans and grasp the real issues. The study ascribed the "spiraling crime rate," which J. Edgar Hoover diligently promotes—with heavy asides to a lax moral climate, to a simple population rise in the crime-prone young age group. In efficient law enforcement agencies, not a lax moral climate or parole judges, abet this crime rate. The study found that the rate and cost of crime will not decrease until research technology is implemented to discourage check forgers and other high cost nuisance or repeater offenders. The lifetime cost within the system of justice for an adult robbery offender is $3,700; for a check forger, $16,900. "We strongly urge a reallocation of resources to handle nuisance offenders in a more suitable, less costly way . . . Special methods are currently available to make it more difficult to steal cars, forge checks and commit burglary, for example," concludes Space-General.

Based on favorable assessments of the studies by his agency heads and by a non-profit corporation (Systems Development Corporation), Governor Brown announced, "We believe the experimental phase of the project is over. In every case, the reports said systems engineering is a feasible approach to the problems at hand. In some cases, the engineers said it was the *only* workable approach." The problem became how to implement this great, promising talent, and at this point, a dilemma faced by California and the rest of the nation emerges. Our government structure mitigates against the best use of our technical and scientific brainpower.

An admittedly simplistic analogy might be in order. What would happen if the various states in the Union were responsible for national security? New York and California might well be duplicating research and development in missile systems. In reality, New York and California aren't duplicating missile efforts, but they quite likely are duplicating research and development efforts in crime prevention, transportation, and sewage disposal.

On a technical basis, there just isn't that much difference between sewage in New York and sewage in California to justify two totally unrelated programs. Carrying the analogy one step further, if the Pentagon approves a missile defense system, it doesn't give the drawings to fifty governors and request that the governors act through their own contracting channels. The Pentagon lets the missile defense system as one prime contract, tailored to take into account variable requirements. Technological development requires great amounts of money, skill, and effort; consolidation of such effort is crucial to success, whether it be eradicating smog or reaching the moon.

Such a consolidation of effort raises another problem. What "trade offs" in democratic procedure may be involved? In the management of space and defense programs, the executive branch often leaves the legislative branch behind in a fog of "take our word for it" confusion. If the states collectively—or through the federal government—mount a unified program on pollution, will engineers be passing public judgment on the eye-irritating quality of smog and the stench of San Francisco Bay? The conduct of California's experimental program is not always too encouraging in this respect. The program was initiated through an executive-branch allocation of state funds. This generated enough legislative pique to doom more systems studies in land conservation, oceanography, and weather forecasting. Norman Peterson, a former Air Force chief scientist and now president of Resource Synergistic Inc., pinpoints another possible fault. "Our living environment should be shaped by a free body of talent working in the open, not under the security of lock and key, or surveillance of security police. To a great extent, the California aerospace studies were shaped by talent immersed in a secure, defense-oriented environment. . . . This has been a false economy. It is a form of technological totalitarianism." Before interviewing the project leader on the crime study (John Kuhn), this writer had to receive a security badge and a security escort.

The deceptive simplicity of the Application Question thus becomes apparent. Moving traffic would seem much easier than moving men to the moon. Technically and, to a degree, fiscally, this is true. But, organizationally, our government structure makes it the other way around. While systems management and technology may be the principal, perhaps only, means of resolving many public problems, our government structure has only faced up to the challenge of absorbing these tools in the field of national security. Democracy begins to mock itself, making the creation of missiles a far easier task than enhancement of the social environment.

Upon completion of the California studies, Governor Brown asked that the principal financier and customer of the aerospace industry, the federal government, begin to tap the full public potential of this industry's technical resources. "Each of the studies California has produced could as easily be applied to any of the other 49 states. Air and water pollution do not respect state boundaries. . . . No state can afford to carry the burden of a fully engineered system in very many problem areas. And even those who could do so should not be asked to, since these studies will be useful in nearly all of the states."

The studies, and Governor Brown's recommendations to the federal government, have achieved considerable recognition. The Ford Foundation contracted with the National Institute of Public Affairs in Washington, D.C. to evaluate the studies. The Institute director confirmed that the California experiment was much more than just an attempt to scare up some more business for Aerojet-General and Lockheed. Reports Dr. Carl Stover, "Without question, the California studies proved the feasibility of bringing industrially-based capabilities in systems analysis, engineering, and management to bear productively in dealing with public problems outside the defense and space programs." The National Association of City Managers, the Council of State Governments, and the Conference of Mayors have all solicited the U.S. Department of

Housing and Urban Development for help in financing systems analysis programs. Bi-partisan interest has been evident. Recently forty-four Republicans in Congress proposed a national commission to help apply systems management "to resolve national and community problems." On the other side of the aisle, Senator Gaylord Nelson, with the support of Senators Clark, McGovern, and Jennings Randolph, has introduced a bill for a five-year, $125,000,000 program in systems management studies. (It is perhaps noteworthy that none of these senators come from a defense-impacted state. Perhaps there is a growing recognition that states have more to gain by diversifying the capabilities of California's aerospace industry than by fighting over shares in the defense pie.) Senator Nelson has dolled up his proposal as a "Space Age Trajectory to the Great Society."

Unfortunately, while the Great Society is in obvious need of some managerial and technical help, its directors have been slow to adopt Senator Nelson's trajectory. Vice President Hubert Humphrey has said some nice words and it is rumored that President Johnson himself requested a copy of the crime study. (The study was released in the wake of the Watts riots and state officials played up the report's ability to pinpoint Watts as a major problem district. The timing of the release and the accompanying puffery—a "plan for conquering crime" prepared by "aerospace engineers whose techniques are conquering space"—suggest that state officials have absorbed some of the aerospace public relations tactics.) Yet executive branch interest in the California experiment, indeed in the basic issues raised by the studies, has not been reflected in any large stir of contract or managerial activity. Noting that many federally-supported "think" factories, like his own, cater almost exclusively to the Pentagon, RAND Corporation president Henry S. Rowen says, "What is needed are centers for the study and analysis of all major social problems. . . . They could bring together and focus the work of analysts now working separately. They could stimulate interest in social problems in analysts not now working on them. And finally they could provide a training ground for analysts who might later work directly in the Government."

With the aid of federal grants, California continues systems studies in welfare programs, a land use study, and a waste disposal study for an urban-agricultural area (Fresno County). The Canadian Ministry of Health has contracted with TRW Systems to do systems work in hospital planning. Look for more federal interest to materialize if the Russian Ministry of Health contracts with TRW Systems.

On the city level, the Department of Housing has awarded a contract to Detroit to develop program budgeting and systems analysis.

The pace of these efforts hardly matches the challenge of bringing American government abreast of the scientific times. A deadly, self-feeding cycle emerges. The more proficient the national security and prestige agencies become at exploiting the prowess of technology, the more they can lay claim to monopolizing our technological resources. Meanwhile, urban renewal, water quality control, and the War on Poverty thrash about amid fragmented funding, direction, and political boundaries.

With the end of the moon race in sight, a splendid opportunity to interrupt this tyrannical cycle and reorder our technological priorities emerges. Yet NASA, with White House approval, is busy developing plans to maintain itself at the level of federal funding it is accustomed to. Aerospace politicians in California eagerly curry a bread and butter follow-up space program. The astronauts who finally reach Mars may well leave their families in a Los Angeles struggling with an eternal traffic jam, coughing on ashen air, and otherwise supporting the space follow-on program.

There are more bread and butter contracts in the offing too. Communist China is conveniently replacing a mellowing Russia as a code word for keeping up the flow of arms contracts; note the renaissance of the anti-missile missile contract. Ocean technology is being recruited as the basis for an inner space race run by multimillion-dollar subs with critical atomic piles. The Navy, as the market analysts say, is where the new production money is. Brain pirates are ignoring retired Air Force generals in favor of retired admirals. Aerospace engineers are once more mum at the family dinner table. Secretary of Defense McNamara's departure is viewed as a possible boon for big defense contracts. In a farewell editorial, *Aerospace Technology* characterized McNamara as an official who catered to mere "product improvement" rather than "innovations in strategic weaponry."

As the prospect for bread and butter contracts brightens, initial aerospace enthusiasm for the California program wanes. Public reference to aerospace involvement in the program is often perfunctory, often exploited by brain pirates in recruiting idealistic or security-minded Ph.D.'s. There are also optimistic name changes. The Winter Convention on Military Electronics is now the Winter Convention on Aerospace and Electronics. Technological fallout remains the aerospace industry's proud contribution to civilian culture in California and the nation at large. Did you know that San Franciscans wear false teeth made from a metal alloy developed for rockets? Did you know that an anti-fog coating for the X-15 plane warms infant cradles in Los Angeles? Do you ever wonder if the space agency would be satisfied to subsist on the technological crumbs from a waste management program? A study prepared for the U.S. Arms Control and Disarmament Agency by Analytical Services Inc. reports, "Increased economic activity in the aerospace industry as a result of Vietnam dissipated much of the industry's interest in early diversification into civilian problems." Since 1965, the level of non-aerospace business performed by the industry has remained almost constant, according to the Aerospace Industries Association.

That a technological reorientation to social problems might cut in on the aerospace industry's bread and butter future inspires second thoughts. *Technology Week* has been an enthusiastic supporter of aerospace systems application, to wit the fine January 23, 1967 issue devoted to "Goals of Technology." Yet *Technology Week* recently felt compelled to unfold a "Space Parable" in its weekly editorial. The unidentified narrator of the parable describes how, in 1968, the President of the United States cuts back on space efforts in favor of urban renewal, civil rights, and other social programs. The narrator says the White House seems to have overlooked the great economic and political strength of the aerospace industry, "both because it was more diffuse and because it was a new political element." As a result of this oversight, aerospace layoffs trigger riots in Downey, California (North American Aviation) that make "Watts a mild incident in comparison." A conservative California governor subsequently defeats the President, vastly increases conventional armament programs, and thus allows Russia to seize a U.S. Manned Orbiting Laboratory with a sophisticated anti-missile weapon. The narrator closes the parable by welcoming the reader to a meeting "of the Supreme Soviet in the Capitol building of the United States Soviet Socialist Republic." As the editorial suggests, the aerospace industry has reached that degree of economic eminence where it can declare "What is good for the aerospace industry is damn good for the United States." This is the creature that the federal government has zealously built up and entrusted with so much of our technological resources.

California has thus supplied a twofold answer to the Application Question. Yes, the technology and technologists we employ in aerospace could be instrumental in resolving major public problems on earth. The trouble is we are making it easier and easier to do the former and harder and harder to do the latter. As a result, the aerospace industry sinks deeper and deeper into the national security rut, taking with it that much-publicized society of the future-perfect, California.

James Schevill

THE CHANGING CALIFORNIA CULTURE

"He's got an eerie sense of reality." I overheard this remark spoken by a bearded young man with long hair, jeans, and sandals at an exhibit of paintings by René Magritte at the University of California. The Magritte show was jammed with visitors, mostly young, who revealed a new sympathy and understanding of the Belgian painter's surrealistic images. Particularly one painting owned by the Museum of Modern Art in New York—"River of Light, II"—received much attention. The painting shows houses at night on a dark, shadowy street illuminated only by the dim glow of a street lamp. Most of the windows in the houses are shuttered dark. A few windows in various homes glitter with hidden, interior light beneath thick trees stretching through the darkness into the sky. The sky! . . . Suddenly one perceives that the sky is brilliant daylight, floating with high clouds. Magritte wrote of this and of other paintings in the series he did around 1950: "An inspired thought combines what was offered to it *in an order evocative of mystery* . . . A thought limited to similarities can only contemplate a starry sky with a nocturnal landscape. An inspired thought which evokes the mystery of a visible thing can be described by painting . . . "

The gap between youth and age that is particularly evident in California today is a gap in vision. The older generation is still largely literal and materialistic in approach. Their thoughts stem from pragmatic, representational considerations. They have little desire to evoke the mystery of visible things. Above all they have a sometime faded, but still active pride in their materialistic system of practical values, their laws, their universities, their institutions. The young have no pride in this adult system and rebel increasingly against the necessity to conform to institutions with which they cannot identify. I am talking about a central split in vision to which there are obviously a vast number of exceptions. Many young people have no desire to revolt and conform instinctively for the sake of jobs and family security. But their conformity is as impassive as a hollow wall. At the slightest provocation cracks of doubt appear. Their values are defensive and skin-deep rather than tenaciously rooted. If they believe, they believe in their jobs, rather than the community in which they live. The pride in community that has always been central to the creation of an important culture is almost totally missing in California.

While accepting and often living on the allowances and gifts of their parents, the young want as Magritte put it, "an order evocative of mystery." They are tired of two-dimensional statesmen in a universe of unknown, changing dimensions. Mysterious titles, questions, and slogans decorate their walls and windows and mark their cars and motorcycles. One day in quick succession I saw "ONDINE SPIRIT" painted on a small red sports car and "SINE QUA NON" lettered on the front of a dusty Volkswagen bus. "SUPPORT ALL THE VARIOUS THINGS," said a casual poster at a recent student election at San Francisco State College. A popular coffee shop in Haight Street in San Francisco where I read my poems some time ago is called THE I AND THOU. The names of the rock and roll bands are in constant competition to catch the skeptical, questioning tone of the scene: The Grateful Dead, The Moby Grape, The 13th Floor Elevators, The Wildflower, The Quicksilver Messenger Service, The Final Solution, Big Brother and the Holding Company, The Jefferson Airplane, The Sopwith Camel, The Lovin' Spoonful. "Make Love, Not War" is more than a cliché that one sees on buttons and posters. It is question, answer, and accusation all in one statement.

The young rebellion travels frequently in long hair, bare feet, and strange costumes not for the sake of the casual, unkempt look as many adults like to think, but as an obvious question of conventional images. What are the conventional images the rebels question? They have their own eerie reality as in the following excerpt from an obituary printed in the San Francisco *Chronicle,* September 27, 1966:

> Dr. Hubert L. Eaton, founder of the vast Forest Lawn Memorial Parks, was entombed yesterday in an elaborately grandiose ceremony climaxed by his formal induction as an immortal of Forest Lawn Memorial Court of Honor.
>
> The spectacle was attended by some 1000 business and cultural leaders and was reminiscent in its sweep and grandeur of some of the funerals for screen stars held at Forest Lawn in years past.
>
> The invited guests included Richard Nixon, Ezra Taft Benson, George Randolph Hearst, Jr., Joe E. Brown, Greer Garson, Ronald Reagan, Conrad Hilton, and opera singer Mary Costa.
>
> The honorary casket bearers included Herbert Hoover, Jr., Walt Disney, Norman Chandler, president of the Los Angeles Times Mirror Company, and such prominent businessmen as Leonard K. Firestone, A. C. Rubel, and Asa V. Call. . . .
>
> The ceremony began with an organ rendition of "March Romaine." Brian Sullivan, the operatic tenor, then sang "Ah Sweet Mystery of Life" accompanied by the Roger Wagner Chorale.

After readings from the Scriptures and a eulogy delivered by former Governor Goodwin Knight, Eaton's name was formally submitted by W. Turney Fox, a retired judge of the Court of Appeals, as an immortal of the Memorial Court of Honor.

Dr. George H. Armacost, president of the University of the Redlands, read a scroll accepting Eaton to Memorial Court, a special chamber of the Hall of the Crucifixion-Resurrection.

Only five previously designated "immortals" are entombed in the room. They include Robert A. Millikan, a Nobel Prize-winning scientist; Carrie Jacobs Bond, a composer of folk songs; and Jan Styka, the artist who painted the crucifixion, a 45-by-195 foot painting that adorns the front of the hall.

I showed this obituary to various students, and their comments came in quick spurts:

"Entombment, why it's old Doc Pharoah Eaton."

"Formal induction as an immortal . . . Who are they kidding?"

"Look at who *they* are, both Reagan and Nixon and all those business men and publishers."

" 'Ah Sweet Mystery of Life' was supposed to be Eaton's favorite tune. Imagine how the Roger Wagner Chorale must have felt singing that sticky marshmallow."

"Somehow you have to admire a man who becomes an 'immortal' in his own cemetery."

"Why didn't the college president give Eaton an honarary Ph.D. when he accepted his body to Memorial Court?"

"The whole Establishment—even a judge to assure a verdict of immortality."

"What about the other immortals—Millikan with Carrie Jacobs Bond and Jan Styka?"

"Who was Styka?"

"He did a 195 foot-long painting of the crucifixion that Eaton exhibited as 'the largest religious painting in the world.' "

"Pretty cool, man, 195 feet of painting. That's like twenty large living rooms. You've got to admit that's real size."

The Forest Lawn tone of size and sentimentality has spread even to Automobile Row in San Francisco. In one agency there is a "Conversationary Gold Room" where presumably customers can engage in golden conversations with salesmen. If the customer wants to buy a secondhand car he can do so with safe prestige in a "Resale Salon." As a uniquely distorted satirical advertising tone shapes the business world increasingly, is it any wonder that a calculated anti-advertising tone shapes the language and attitudes of the young generation? In San Francisco an artist named Wes Wilson has created a series of unusual posters advertising mainly rock and roll dances. Instead of following the traditional advertising rule of clear, visible letters and numbers announcing time, place, and performers, Wilson's posters are often extremely difficult to read. He uses swirling, circling Op-Art patterns so that colors and lettering merge. Many of his posters have the attraction of inscrutable, entertaining color mazes.

If the tone of life in California is an increasingly eerie reality, it is easy to perceive a central cause. A state that is absorbing thousands of newcomers every day cannot maintain any standards of continuity. Size has become the determining factor of existence. Suburbs rise and rise, complacent and similar on the surface, affluent with patches of front lawn, trees, backyards, and two-car garages, but all purchased on long-term mortgages. The majority of the adult population live leashed to banks and loan companies, dependent on fixed salaries and regular incomes to pay off their obligations. The smoke of backyard barbecues, the fever of weekend fishing and camping escapes, the endless, relentless pressure of long distance freeway commuting through growing traffic snarls, mark the restrained passion of these suburban lives.

The isolation of the suburbs is inextricably connected with the boom of specialized technology, particularly in Southern California which is now the world's largest missile center and the landscape of a rapidly spreading aerospace industry. Los Angeles has become the focus of economic and cultural power in the state, but it remains to be seen whether its increasingly disjointed surburban makeup will permit the unity that is essential to create a stable audience for the arts. Thus far the new Music Center, with its concert hall and projected theaters, and the new Art Museum several miles away, represent the luxurious avocation of wealth more than the vocation of contemporary creativity.

Artistic experiment is hardly possible in the rootless, anonymous surburban environments created for middle-aged jobholders or retired oldsters, so it is apparent why the rebellion in California is centered in young people. The suburban dwellers live an eerie reality of conformity, mainly separate white communities complete with all possible gadgets available in local supermarkets and drug stores, all whitewashed with a false sense of comfortable cultural leisure. False because these communities offer mainly sports and countless television antennae for entertainment as opposed to the more unified and centralized pleasures in the big cities with their museums, libraries, galleries, bookstores, coffee shops, and theaters, however inadequate these facilities may be. It is no wonder that young people suddenly find themselves bored with the plainness and the similarity of suburban "entertainment" and flock in increasing numbers to create small bohemian centers in the cities.

As with many other concepts, the word "entertainment" is suffering a sea change. In recent years entertainment has come to mean something evanescent, unimportant, a play that runs for a while on Broadway and is quickly forgotten, a one-shot television broadcast, a film that flickers on screens for a few weeks and is then buried in a can in a bank vault. What does entertainment really mean? Entertain—from the Latin *inter,* between, and *tenere,* to hold—meaning in its root action simply a contact between performer and audience and the holding of that contact. The *holding* quality of the word has been forgotten. Many young people have discovered that real entertainment has nothing to do with passivity or indifference. Real entertainment awakes, excites, endures, holds. What kind of pleasure is it that has no enduring values? The revolt, even if largely unconscious, grows against media that depersonalize and institutionalize entertainment. Certainly the revolt may be relatively small in numbers, but where cultural developments are concerned it is not necessarily statistics that count, contrary to the claims of many social scientists. The spark of imagination may set off fires in any direction.

Take the case of Ken Kesey. Some years ago, before his current difficulties with the law I heard him speak at San Francisco State College. He said that he no longer considered himself to be a writer and he was interested in new methods of expression, particularly film-making. Writing seemed to him basically "imitative" and therefore out of date. Why do young people feel that film is the most interesting and significant of all art forms? In May, 1966 in *Cahiers du Cinéma*, Robert Bresson, the French film director, said in an interview with another leading film director, Jean-Luc Godard: "Soon they [the arts] will not exist. But strangely enough, if they are killed by cinema, radio and television, the very arts that kill them will end up by making art anew." If there is a mystique in this claim that seems hard to justify, as it represents the natural bias of a film-maker, it is nevertheless the mystique of many young creative talents. The allure of films is not only in sensuous, immediate images that can be photographed, but in the blur of consciousness, the rhythms of chaos, that film can depict more easily and more convincingly than any other artistic medium today. The young see and hear in films the rhythms and images of their lives. Countless film clubs and film projects throughout California, far removed from the professional film orbit in Hollywood, attest to this fact.

Films also relate more easily and directly to the drug scene than other arts. Somehow the technique of cutting and creating a dissociated pattern of images in a film seems closer to the experience of "the expansion of consciousness" that many people claim results from taking the various psychedelic drugs. However, the drug scene too is changing rapidly. "Pot Is Fun" is painted on a stone along the roadside in Big Sur high above the ocean. A popular bumper sticker reads, "Keep California Green—Legalize Grass."

If marijuana is considered less dangerous than alcohol among young people, many of whom have been exposed to the paradox of heavy-drinking, conservative relatives who pontificate against the danger of "drugs" through alcoholic breaths, LSD is becoming less fashionable. The dangers of LSD and of such drugs as methedrine are more apparent. Too many "acid heads" who once displayed creative talent are walking around as visible displays of the risk when these drugs are taken. Kesey has played a large part of this scene. Although his announced "Graduation Ceremony" at Winterland in San Francisco, at which users of LSD were to "graduate from acid," failed to come off and a small, relatively private ceremony was substituted, there is no doubt that a counter-movement against the indiscriminate use of drugs is beginning to have a strong influence. Lew Welch, reading at the Poetry Center's fall, 1966, series in San Francisco, began with praise for Kesey and his "Graduation Ceremony." Welch said that what he admired about Kesey was the sense of a "man walking tall" in a time when the major situation in literature seemed to be that of "a man losing all the time." In a program note, Welch also defended the young generation:

> Happily, I'm still alive and am just turned 40. From such a rare height it is possible to say (in defense of my work, and others here or gone), that today, foolish as they may appear to the frightened eye, young America swings much harder than we did, with less fear, and more love.

"Less fear and more love." There is a new sense of commitment among the young. It is particularly obvious in the relationship between the arts and the civil rights movement. Various active workers in the civil rights movement with whom I have spoken all tend to feel uneasy about the "love movement" among the young. They have had too many bitter, practical experiences of the compromise necessary to make any progress at all in urban race relationships to feel that the "love movement" has any real meaning. Yet Stokely Carmichael wrote in *The New York Review of Books,* September 22, 1966:

> The society we seek to build among black people, then, is not a capitalist one. It is a society in which the spirit of community and humanistic love prevail. The word love is suspect; black expectations of what it might produce have been betrayed too often. But those were expectations of a response from the white community, which failed us. The love we seek to encourage is within the black community, the only American community where men call each other "brother" when they meet. We can build a community of love only where we have the ability and power to do so: among blacks.

When Carmichael spoke at the University of California, thousands of people, white and black, gave him a standing ovation. In his talk he stated that he was not a racist, spoke of his belief in integration and his friendship with many whites, but also emphasized again his firm belief in "black power" as the only way to work for Negro rights. The newspapers that I read distorted completely the tone of his remarks. The press in California cannot escape responsibility for its share in the "white backlash" that contributed to the election of Ronald Reagan as governor. As one young Negro leader in the Anti-Poverty Program said bitterly during the "riots" in San Francisco, "The newspapers want to make a big thing about Black Power with capital letters and revolution. When we try to get all kinds of cultural events going in the ghetto areas, the newspapers don't even bother to report them. But when a little bitter action occurs to try and break down some of the ghetto isolation, the newspapers act like it's an invasion of the white community. All they think of is selling papers."

The close connection between the civil rights movement, the fear and backlash against this movement, and the rebellion of the young is extremely clear. As the splintered violence of our society increases, the young increasingly adopt the masks of "love" and "peace," as forms of ironic protest as much as forms of belief. One day my daughter's dog came home from his daily downtown trip with a button "Join The Peace Brigades" fastened to his collar. "Liberty is the color of night," wrote Jean-Paul Sartre in an essay on "Negritude." Many young people today believe that the only way to find a culture of freedom is to explore the real color of blackness and fight against the white fear that is part of the growing suburban isolation in California. A talented young Negro playwright, Marvin Jackmon, while at San Francisco State College, wrote in a paper "Toward A Theater of Blackness":

> I am searching for the mode of artistic presentation that will best serve the needs of Afro-America in its struggle for human dignity . . . Negritude is the universal experience of blackness—it is the Black Tradition, the Black Mythology . . . In terms of dramatic form, Negritude is akin to Greek comedy—for Negritude affirms life ('Keep on pushing, Brother, everything's gonna be all right later on'); it affirms the dignity of the human personality, of universal brotherhood.

An important development in theater in the San Francisco Bay Area has been the establishment of several Negro theater groups. From November 11 through November 14, 1966, at the Hunters Point Art Fair and Festival, several of these groups including the Black Arts–West, the Aldridge Players, the San Francisco Playwrights' Workshop Company, and the Black Players presented scenes and plays by LeRoi Jones, Marvin Jackmon, Ed Bullins, Langston Hughes, Lorraine Hansberry, and Ossie Davis. The orientation of these groups covers the spectrum of the civil rights movement, from collaboration and inter-casting with whites in the production of classical plays to an exclusive focus on black problems and "black power."

Perhaps the most far-reaching effects of the changing California culture will be in education. No longer is the campus an isolated community set apart from family and society for the purpose of a rational training and investigation of facts and professions. The secondary schools as well as the colleges and universities are becoming more involved in new methods of teaching the arts and sciences. Dr. Herbert Wong, principal of the Washington School in Berkeley, because of his interest and experience in the jazz world as a "disc jockey," has created a fascinating series of jazz programs in his school that demonstrate the value of bringing in important musicians such as Oscar Peterson to give the school situation a new dimension in creativity. The Poetry Center, under a grant from the Rosenberg Foundation, is conducting a series of programs in various secondary schools throughout the San Francisco Bay Area that lift language off the dull pages of textbooks and show the living excitement of rhythms and images when they sound in the ear and echo in the mind. With a grant from the National Foundation on the Arts and the help of the California Arts Commission, the San Francisco Opera has formed a touring company called the Western Opera Theatre to perform in schools and communities that have rarely been exposed to opera. As yet the possibilities of federal and state aid to the arts in California suffer from a lack of creative unity of purpose in artistic circles and the usual malaise of administrative bureaucracy that spends more time on red tape than on creative programs.

The development of Experimental Colleges is most representative of the revolution in progress. At San Francisco State College, the rapidly growing Experimental College is called by many students "the Quiet Revolution." In recent years the Associated Students of the college have become interested in financing significant educational and cultural programs rather than in merely supporting the familiar student sports and relaxing entertainments that characterize so many campuses. With the increasing size of colleges and universities in California, it has become apparent that student bodies, through such means as student body cards, bookstores, and other income sources, have financial resources for almost any kind of activities they are permitted to undertake. At San Francisco State, the students have financed such events as contemporary arts festivals; a Tutorial Program in which over two hundred students are helping underprivileged children throughout the city; guest lectures on almost any conceivable subject; a film on the poet, Theodore Roethke, made by David Myers and produced by the Poetry Center; various series of film showings; and a weekend of spontaneous happenings, light shows, rock and roll dances, music, and theatrical presentations called "Whatever It Is." Now the student body is budgeting large amounts of money for the Experimental College.

The Experimental College began to take form during the spring term of 1966. The administrative machinery was developed, nineteen seminars were organized, and the writer, Paul Goodman, was hired as the first visiting professor to be paid by the students. By the fall of 1966 the Experimental College had burgeoned into more than sixty courses with an enrollment of over nine hundred students. The subject matter varied from familiar surveys designed to fill gaps in departmental curriculum offerings, such as "Music Since 1945," to courses with new metaphysical and social overtones, such as "Propaganda, Brainwashing, and the Political Metaphor," "Art: The Super-Present," and "Dance of Joy: Seminar in the Ecstatic Style of Cosmic Consciousness." Russell Bass, the editor of a new San Francisco magazine called *Context,* described the Experimental College in his first issue:

> The Experimental College is not a building or a plot of ground, but it is a space—a human space. The chief concern of the Experimental College, as I know it and have been touched by it, is the architecture of human space.
>
> How do we fashion our lives and the architecture of our space so that the aspirations of our secret moments may be fulfilled? It has been charged by many students that colleges concern themselves too heavily with matters of the mind and too little with matters of the heart. . . .
>
> The colleges and universities sometimes help people learn to think, but seldom what to think about. Attention to feeling and belief is thwarted by the grading system, and by the way people are labeled student, teacher, or administrator. The conflict between a college demanding only thought, and a heart that feels and must feel, is the source of much of the discontent on college

campuses. The need to feel and the need to think are seldom
given appropriate space. And the knowledge of how to bring
those needs into a proper relationship is seldom taught.

Here is the crux of the matter—the widespread feeling of young
people that they must find an appropriate space and balance for
their need to feel and to think. If the need for feeling, for "love,"
is uppermost in the demands of the young generation, the reason
is clear. Colleges and "multiversities" have grown too large to
honor any close relationship between teacher and student. A dry
delivery and memorizing of facts in ever-larger lecture classes have
often substituted for a true atmosphere of investigation possible
only in small classes where student and teacher benefit equally
from a climate of humility in the pursuit of truth. The arrogance
of our educators and administrators—many of them hiding, alas,
behind the shields of liberalism—has led them into an increasing
defense of size, a demand for more and more and more of everything which has trapped them into a merely defensive position.
Like the backers of the new cultural centers, these educators and
administrators find themselves fighting mainly for real estate and
budgets and have little time to spare for creativity.

Where will the new search for feeling, for "love," lead? What
"architecture of human space" can emerge in a California, incredi-
bly wealthy, but badly fragmented politically and culturally?
When Léopold Sédar Senghor, the African poet and President of
Senegal, visited San Francisco, one of his expressed desires was
to meet with writers as well as the usual political figures. To
these writers he expressed his faith in a "new humanism" that was
growing throughout the world, in the interchange of ideas and
feelings among all the peoples of the world. In one of his poems
Senghor writes:

> . . . Master of the Initiates, I know I need your wisdom to break
> the cypher of things
> To learn my office as father . . .
> To measure exactly the field of my duties, to share out the
> harvest forgetting neither worker nor orphan.

> The song is not only a charm, by it the woolly heads of my
> flock are fed.
> The poem is bird-serpent, marriage of shadow and dawnlight
> The Phoenix rises, he sings with wings extended, over
> the carnage of words.

The literal word, having failed in its suggestive power, is being destroyed to be created anew. "Love Is The Enemy" reads the legend on the back of a battered multicolored car I saw driving down the California coast. It takes little knowledge of the scene to realize that this means that the young "Enemy" our society is confronting is "Love." "Eat More Art" was lettered on a screen at the back of the stage during one of the weekend fairs in October sponsored by the Artists' Liberation Front, a group formed to challenge the city's hierarchy in the arts. The obvious danger of the spirited youthful rebellion is that it will end in an irony of nihilism caused by the failure to balance the search for feeling with the discovery of reason. Those who merely revolt from the American industrial tradition of literal materialism soon find out that they cannot make a false separation between feeling and idea. If we feel and fear the coldness of abstract intellectual ideas that torment humanity, we must also feel and fear the furnace of abstract passions that lock mankind into a false subjectivity and prevent the creation of a real community in which feeling and thought are balanced for the welfare of all. California is in the throes of astonishing births and agonizing deaths which are often hard to distinguish. What is clear is that the revolution of youth will not be stopped.

In November, 1966, Martha Graham and her remarkable company visited San Francisco and demonstrated the dedication and the standards that must prevail in the arts if an enduring culture is to be achieved. In a superb conception of the trials and glories of the creative imagination, "The Acrobats of God," in which she appears herself looking back with humorous wisdom and tenacious endurance over a lifetime of frustration and triumph in the dance, she testifies to the ultimate union of intuition and thought. Using

the metaphor of the early Church Fathers who subjected themselves to the discipline of the desert and were called the athletes
of God, she celebrates with rare humor and maturity the nature of
the dance. She shows how the thrust of the body toward freedom
is impossible unless a disciplined imagination combines with an
experienced idea. It was no accident that all of her performances
were completely sold out and many young people attended and
gave her standing ovations. In the prevailing California climate
of restless and superficial eerie reality, she proved the magic and
hope of Senghor's Phoenix rising, "with wings extended, over the
carnage of words."

Theodore Roszak

LIFE IN THE

INSTANT CITIES

Well over one hundred "new towns" of one description or another are presently under construction or in the planning stage in the United States. More than one-third of them are in California, and it is likely that the state will continue to dominate these efforts at shoring up the disintegration of American cities. California's seemingly uncheckable population boom; its citizens' masochistic fascination with the agony of freeway commuting; the pre-eminence in California's economy of light industry which can locate almost anywhere; the vast accessibility of California land to speculators and private developers—these factors will probably continue to invite and encourage new town and satellite city developments in California.

There is also the fact that urban sprawl and blight seem to be far more hideously advanced in California than any place else on earth. Or perhaps that is only an illusion created by one's constant realization that this is quite simply one of the loveliest pieces of landscape and climate in the world. There is so much more natural beauty to be destroyed in California—and it *is* being destroyed before one's eyes with a grim nihilistic insistence that approaches the demonic. It is almost as if California had been created to demonstrate how boorish and wantonly wasteful human beings can be: a beautiful face on which the scars of a sadistic crime can show more vividly. Day by day, one can observe the decay spreading—and it spreads from the cities, traveling at a mile-a-minute along the great highways that lie across the land like welts on a beaten body. The groves and woods, seascapes and gentle hills are mercilessly planed away and squared off to make place for exotically named tracts of pastel-colored cracker-box homes clustered around a quaint, or folksy, or garish shopping center that is always the same assemblage of chain store operations. And between the tracts, along the highways, like cancer seeping along the lymph ducts of a stricken organism, the "slurb" sets in: a billboarded and neon-lit honky-tonk of gas stations, hot-dog stands, drive-in movies, secondhand tire stores, junkyards, pizza parlors, motels. . . . Then, soon enough, the smog comes, settling in like an act of ecological incorporation that makes the tract or town an official part of California urban life.

Surely no piece of land has been so grotesquely raped as the once magnificent Pacific sea coast running south along the San Francisco peninsula. It is now an unsightly scab of congested tracts and slurb-lined freeway. One gazes at this horror and, knowing it is only one small sample of what is happening everywhere in the state, one realizes beyond all doubt why all these people have come so eagerly to California. It is for one single-minded reason: not to find comfort and loveliness, but to violate and make ugly beyond repair. And in how many of these cases has the destruction been for nothing better than to create ghost towns? In some of the cheaper and more hideous San Francisco

Bay Area tracts (they bear names like "Tropicana Village" or "Eden Roc" or "Olé!") down-payments and terms are so low that transient families can buy, move in, dilapidate, and then abandon the property, and vanish. It is an open secret that many areas of California are grossly overbuilt with such tracts already and that both savings and loans associations and developers are sweating to save sour investments. (See "The Easy Lenders" by Michael Harris; *The Nation,* August 22, 1966.)

At this point, there is nothing worth mentioning in the way of an enforceable official program or an active public agency that stands in the path of this statewide devastation. So, by default, some of the very few efforts one can discern to plan and direct the chaotic growth of California have emerged from the ranks of the real estate interests themselves. It is certainly the most significant single aspect of the new towns—not only in California, but across the nation—that the developments are the product of private planning and investment. In marked contrast to the British and Scandinavian new towns, most of which are government undertakings from first to last, the American new towns are an effort by private capital to solve the problem of urban decay. Which means that the solution is being undertaken by way of making a handsome profit. One might therefore suspect from the outset that, in this instance as in so many others, public good and private gain simply won't mix and no better than a bad compromise between the two will result. And, ultimately, I think the suspicion is justified.

The two most ambitious new towns that are presently under construction in California are Foster City, located about twenty miles south of San Francisco on the San Francisco peninsula, and Valencia, in the San Fernando Valley north of Los Angeles. Another as yet unnamed town, which is far larger and in some respects more interesting than either of these, but which is still very much in the planning stage, will rise on the 88,000-acre Irvine ranch east of Los Angeles and will use a new branch of the University of California as the economic core for its projected 500,000 population. Most of the other California new towns seem to be either little more than glorified housing tracts–cum–shopping centers, or well-to-do old folks towns, like the various Leisure World developments, and are too trivial or too eccentric to merit much attention as efforts at city planning.

But both Valencia and Foster City are experiments in privatized town planning that deserve to be taken seriously—if for no other reason than that they take themselves so very seriously. Both are comparable to Robert Simon's Reston in Virginia and Edward Rause's Columbia in Maryland. Both purport to be conscientious attempts to inhibit urban blight by achieving Ebenezer Howard's vision of the garden city. Indeed, Howard's idea of the self-contained satellite town—totally planned from the beginning, embracing all the vital services of a community and supported by its own economic base—is frequently referred to in the literature for both towns.

Valencia, whose designer is Victor Gruen and Associates, is the more grandiose effort of the two, though Foster City is further along in the building. (There are already 4,000 people living there.) The site for Valencia is the 44,000-acre Newhall ranch (about twenty miles north of Burbank and presently inhabited by many cattle and a few hundred oil wells). This ranch, larger in size than the city of San Francisco, is the prime holding of the multibillion dollar Newhall Land and Farming Company, which owns 150,000 acres scattered over nine ranches in California. The plans for Valencia call for a city of 200,000 to 250,000 population by 1990, largely supported by its own industrial park. This along with Irvine is by far the largest new town development in America, dwarfing even Reston which is planned for 75,000 inhabitants on 6,750 acres—and much more so Foster City, which is expected to have a population of only 35,000 on 2,600 acres by 1974. (Foster City, however, more nearly approaches the dimensions of Howard's classic garden city—which was planned for 32,000 people.)

Foster City takes its uninspired but no doubt ego-gratifying name from T. Jack Foster, an Oklahoma land developer who boasts of owning the tallest building on the Waikiki skyline in Honolulu (named, of course, the Foster Tower Hotel. In Oklahoma, if you own it, you put your brand on it.) In the early sixties Foster bought Brewer Island, a swampy grazing area in San Francisco Bay just east of San Mateo, filled it in here and there, diked up the Bay to form lagoons and canals, and set about investing a half billion dollars in "a new kind of metropolis, pre-planned every step of the way." The promotional literature for Foster City gushes something awful—and insists on exaggerating the community into a "metropolis" when it isn't calling it a "dream." For example:

> In the age of many miracles wouldn't it be infinitely better to dream-build a new city than to redesign and over-extend an old one? . . . Can a dream like this become a reality? Yes, indeed! At this very moment the dream of a perfect city is being translated into steel and wood, concrete and glass. This is Foster City, a daring concept of an all-inclusive, self-supporting urban community. This is Foster City where a man may build his castle and raise his family in the finest of all possible worlds! . . . Foster City—a need fulfilled—a dream come true, thanks to the vision, enthusiasm and courage of T. Jack Foster, financier and major developer, and his sons.

The subtitle of this epic is "the island of blue lagoons." Well, what can rhetoric like that do but make one doubt the seriousness and good sense of the whole project? Still, Foster City requires attention because it is an example of what new town building has come to mean among private builders—and through them to the public at large. Foster City was, for example, the subject of a special and very ambitious exhibition in 1965 at the San Francisco Museum of Art. So to a large part of the Bay Area public Foster City represents what the new town is. Unfortunately, the first thing one notes about the project is how much of the Madison Avenue mentality clings to what purports to be a sober attempt to solve a major social problem. And this is also revealing of many of the gravest weaknesses of profit-based town planning.

But before turning to those weaknesses, let us see first what there is to be said in favor of instant cities like Valencia and Foster City—both of which boast of having been two whole years in the planning. I think there are two points to be credited to their planners. To begin with, in both cases (as in Reston and Columbia) we have, at least in theory, a deliberate effort to break away from the depressing dormitory suburb and to turn instead toward a more organically planned community. The Valencia developers put it this way:

> Parts of the Valley could be profitably turned over to tract developers and become an extension, in style and function, of the variegated sub-cities and "bedroom" towns of the San Fernando Valley. Or they [the developers] could elect to create an island of reason in the path of the metropolitan sprawl. . . . Once having rejected the attractions of the conventional sub-division, the builders are committed to a city. A city which will never need the violent therapy of rebuilding.

What this means, in effect, is that both Foster City and Valencia hope to see a major portion of their populations employed in local business and industry. So a large portion of each site has been set aside and planned for industrial parks. Of the first 4,000 acres of Valencia to be developed, a concentrated 600 acres will go to industrial uses. Of the 2,600 initial acres of Foster City now under development, 310 are reserved for industry. While none of the new towns intend to include Ebenezer Howard's provisions for some small amount of farming, (a picturesque notion that is probably irrelevant in twentieth-century America anyway, except as a kind of purely artificial amusement for the community) this is clearly a closer approach to garden city autonomy than most of our present suburban developments can claim to be, at least as far as planning goes. I believe there are reasons why this objective will prove difficult to achieve. But it is commendable that, at least on the drawing board, developers recognize the need to dam up the urban sprawl and to diminish commuting by building towns in which residence and employment are combined. This would be especially welcome in the San Fernando Valley where 60-mile commutes (one way) are now common, and where congested eight- and ten-lane freeways during the almost perpetual rush hour look like something out of Dante's *Inferno*.

The rest of what is good about the new towns can be summed up under the heading of physical planning. One need only survey the plans for Valencia or walk a few streets in Foster City to realize that in these projects private developers have come a long way since Charles Levitt soon after World War II set about turning his desolate New Jersey tracts into a Chirico-like nightmare: hundreds of fragile and identical match-box homes crowded into a monotonous concrete and asphalt grid. Both Valencia and Foster City have promised to make allowance for variety, recreational space, intelligent traffic control, and some sense of neighborhood. On the last point—the sense of neighborhood—the literature of the two developments reaches some very high-sounding sociological eloquence. Valencia's literature puts it this way:

> Of special concern to the planner of Valencia is an environmental answer to the restoration of *neighborhoods*, those comfortable clusters ideally comprised of compatible humans with similar ideals and goals, which deliberately and by design include both interdependence and privacy. Webster described neighborhood as 'neighborly disposition or relations, esp. of kindness and good will; neighborliness.' The definition ends sadly '(now rare).' So rare, indeed, that volumes of sociological literature lament the destruction of this classic unit of urban and suburban life. . . . The builders of Valencia . . . have determined to restore the neighborhood.

This act of heroic restoration is understood to have to do with the control of traffic and the location of plazas, schools, churches, malls, etc.

Thus, at least the physical form of neighborhoods has been drawn into the plans of the new towns. The main civic center of Valencia is to be surrounded by "villages," each with a population of 6,000. And, in turn, each village is to be composed of "neighborhoods" of 200 to 700. Foster City will comprise nine "neighborhoods" of about 4,000 each. It must be noted, however, (and we will come back to this point) that these smaller component communities are defined almost entirely by their physical planning, not by social integrity. They are not primarily conceived of as political units. In the case of Valencia, the neighborhoods are ringed about by the open spaces and lakes: again, a physical device which looks pretty on the drawing board, but which guarantees nothing socially.

As for variety and visual appeal, the towns achieve this by providing for a great deal of open space (a very great deal more in the plans for Valencia than for Foster City), parks, malls, riding trails, lakes and lagoons. Auto traffic is intelligently controlled to allow for a good deal of uninterrupted foot traffic—especially in Valencia, where, supposedly, children may walk to schools and stores without having to cross streets. Valencia may also include some form of electric go-cart transport for its malls and a bit of public transportation to and from the civic center. Foster City is built around a winding canal which is supposed to carry a certain amount of picturesque boating.

The commercial and residential architecture also contributes to the planned variety. There will be high-rise civic centers—in Foster City including two great glass boxes by Mies van der Rohe. As for the homes, each town is employing a number of builders, and each builder is providing a selection of styles based on price range. The base price for homes in both towns will apparently be about $22,000–$25,000 (this for very "compact" homes, apparently intended for "retired couples"), and will slope up steeply from there to perhaps $60,000 homes in Foster City and what are called "estate-size ranchos" in Valencia. There are also apartment house accommodations in both towns. These are lavish "garden apartment" arrangements (clusters of buildings connected by a continuous lawn and built around a club-like recreation center: pool, sauna bath, putting green, etc.). Rentals for two bedroom apartments price up from just over $200 per month.

One sees at once that whatever architectural variety this may lead to, such prices screen out immediately one kind of social variety: namely, low income families. Whatever Foster City means when it speaks of "a balanced community," we are still dealing here, as in most new towns, with developments that are very middle, upper-middle class in character. (The price range in Reston, for example, is $27,000 to $46,000.) Neither the Valencia nor Foster City developers seem to want to be frank about that. And in fact, Valencia's literature indulges in some very disreputable propagandizing in this respect. We are told that

> The rationale for the Valencia plan revolves on a uniquely American idea—freedom of choice. . . . The selection of housing within the community will meet the needs of the clerk and the corporate president. . . . This wide-choice thesis was the principal guide in the evolution of the master plan.

This conception of "free choice" reminds one of Anatole France's bitter quip about the law, which, in its even-handed justice, forbids the rich as well as the poor to sleep under bridges and in the streets. In Valencia, we see the poor as well as the rich are completely free to purchase "estate-size ranchos." Both towns stand completely open to anyone, from any walk of life, even the lowly "clerk"—provided he can get up the price. Which is, indeed, "a uniquely American idea" of freedom.

And finally, to finish off what there is to be said in behalf of physical planning: all the basic facilities of the towns have been provided in advance of the building. Both towns provide for sewers, not septic tanks, and both have buried their power lines to eliminate telephone poles and power pylons. Such are the best points in the plans for Valencia and Foster City. Put them all together and what they promise to prospective inhabitants—and this is by far the major emphasis of all the literature for the two towns—is a life of self-contained comfort, active leisure, lavish recreation, luxury, and status. The promotional pictures show us happy families putting out for an afternoon sail on the lake or lagoon, children scampering barefoot through groves of fruit trees, housewives strolling about elegant shopping centers, patio barbeques, esplanades, horse-back riding, swimming pool parties, "flower-splashed malls," golf courses, tennis courts. . . . "The finest of all possible worlds (exclamation point)." And that, we may take it, is what these new towns are meant to be all about: such is their vision of the good life.

Unfortunately a bit of the luster has to be rubbed off this sybaritic image at once. The promotional literature leaves many things very much out of its account—and quite understandably. There is, for example, the fact that the whole of Foster City lies just south of San Francisco Airport and directly in the flight pattern. The island of blue lagoons will thus be treated to the stimulating sounds of the jet age by day and night. And when the airport is opened up to the new supersonics, the community should acquire all the charm of living next to the old Third Avenue "El" in New York. Or, take those quaint Foster City lagoons and canals. They are pleasant enough to look at, but clearly their uses are limited. San Francisco Bay is a lovely place to do some ambitious sailing. But Foster City's little canals are to real sailing as miniature golf is to real golf. What kind of boat does a Foster City-ite buy: a real boat for the Bay, or a toy one for the canals? For the canals will clearly only take tiny, single-sail rigs. And even so their feasibility as a means of internal transportation is dubious. The Safeway shopping center that has already been built in Foster City is called, charmingly, "The Port of Call" and actually has (as the Town Center itself will have) a "parking lot for sailboats (exclamation point)." But the vision of suburban housewives setting sail for the Safeway to pick up five pounds of sugar, jockeying their little rigs along winding canals in those brisk breezes that come darting off the Bay, is something that belongs in a Jacques Tati movie.

Indeed, the compulsive thrust toward prestige and leisure tends, in Foster City as in most contemporary American housing developments, to undercut economic value. Home construction often sacrifices finishing and workmanship and even sensible design in favor of lavish effects and cut-rate luxury. Clearly builders feel that what sells a house these days is the sunken Roman tub, the spacious "family room," the built in wet-bar, the "Queen-size" antiqued mirrors, the onyx-tiled entries, the double pullman sinks, the breakfast bar, the intercom, hi-fi, stereo sound systems, the built-in electric kitchen (the latter must certainly be the only way that pernicious instrument called the electric range can manage to get itself sold any longer). The builders are probably right. Just as the garden apartment designers are probably right in believing that people will forego adequate sound-proofing and privacy to have the inevitable wall-to-wall carpet and garbage disposal. Edward Stone has designed for Foster City a monstrously congested and institutional apartment project called The Commodore (2 bedrooms: $225; 3 bedrooms: $295 per month). But it will doubtless make its way on its attached putting green and swimming pools, which belong to "the Club." The rent at the Commodore automatically admits one to the "Racquet Club"—"all the fun of a resort combined with the privacy of a fashionable club. Can you imagine a better place to entertain your less fortunate friends living in the city?"

More serious than the skimping on construction is the fact that whenever the mortgage bankers behind the new towns feel they must squeeze a nickel, it is the recreational amenities and the more imaginative architects that prove most vulnerable to profit-taking economies. Or, so I understand from people who have been in on the planning at Valencia—where apparently there have been serious second thoughts about all those big parks and artificial lakes. It will be interesting to see, as village follows village into construction at Valencia, how the profits of the last development affect the size of plazas and esplanades in the next.

Now no doubt the physical planning in these developments will always preserve a great deal more in the way of open space, eye-appeal and recreation than is usual in conventional housing tracts. Still, one must recognize that it is not in the least remarkable that a development pitched at this income level should be able to provide such attractions. After all, a suburban location most of whose homes sell in the $30,000–$40,000 bracket and whose family rentals price up from $225 a month, had better be able to provide a good deal more in the way of setting and conveniences than a "$99 down moves you in" housing tract. The critical question about new towns like Valencia and Foster City is, obviously, are they going to be anything *more* than the usual sanitized suburban reservation, but a bit more highly priced? That is: are they going to be *real* garden cities? Are they going to help solve the problem of urban decay? And, above all, what will their quality of life be? Will they overcome the social sameness and malaise of spirit that has come to characterize conventional suburbia? I think the answers to all these questions are bleak. And the reason for pessimism is that the American new towns are, in the last analysis, private, profit-making ventures, undertaken by men who seem driven by force of habit to seek still another buck. And who want to find it soon.

One begins to sense the underlying ambiguity of Valencia and Foster City as soon as one sees how persistently their promotional literature emphasises ease of commuting from the towns. The towns, one is assured, are never more than twenty or thirty minutes from anywhere one might want to get. Freeways are drawn in heavily on all the plans. One hears very quickly, for example, that Foster City is only twenty minutes from San Francisco by the Bayshore freeway . . . only fifteen minutes from Hayward or twenty minutes from Oakland by the new San Mateo Bridge . . .

and that there are even plans for a brand new freeway to San Francisco that will apparently run up the Bay along the whole eastern side of Foster City. (It is unclear how this freeway will affect those whose rather expensive properties now front the Bay and who apparently feel they possess a valuable view—or indeed how it will affect access to the Bay for all the City's would-be yachtsmen. Perhaps the highway commissioners will elevate the road to allow an underpass for sailboats . . .?)

What is the importance of all these commuting facilities to a "prospective 'self-contained' town"? The answer is clear if one does a bit of make-believe househunting in Foster City. Wherever you say your place of work is, a realtor will be sure to tell you Foster City is "near in," and that a great many people in the development are commuting that far and farther. If you want to buy, they want to sell—and who cares about "self-containment"? Can one realistically expect a realtor to turn down a sale because the prospect doesn't plan to work in the nearby industrial park? And, in any case, the industrial park is only partially rented and still a-building. How long can he wait for employees to start arriving? In brief, how does the residence-employment balance get worked out? Who is responsible for making sure self-containment comes about? Or does it really matter? Surely one doesn't get self-containment simply because Victor Gruen has drawn a blue area on a map next to a yellow area, and labeled the one "industrial" and the other "residential."

There are other problems about self-containment. In Valencia the largest single prospective employer at this point is Lockheed. But there seems to be some doubt that Valencia housing will be within reach of many Lockheed employees unless the costs fall under $200 per month. And if Lockheed people will have difficulty reaching the base price on housing, what about the thousands whose semi-skilled or unskilled daily labor and services will be indispensable to a town of 200,000? Valencia is not a community in which shop assistants and shipping clerks, repairmen, policemen, firemen, barbers and beauticians, maintenance men, trash collectors, gardeners, bank tellers, service station attendants and mechanics, waiters and waitresses—or for that matter even lower paid professionals such as teachers, nurses or librarians—could expect to live. Where will they live then? Back in the central city? Or perhaps somewhere nearby, in the nearest low to middle income tract: Valencia's own suburb? Without careful planning and co-ordination one can easily imagine a development as large as Valencia expects to be, experiencing two-way commuting every morning. Out go all the Valencia bread-winners (upper-income professionals, junior and senior executives, engineers) whose work is not in the industrial park; in comes the cheap help to keep the city serviced. Such a system could certainly work; but it has nothing to do with solving the dilemmas of conurbation and the proliferation of freeways.

One begins to suspect that only under government direction can a real garden city be built. For perhaps only a public agency can successfully co-ordinate population with industry. (Indeed in some of the new towns it is an indirect helping hand from Washington that has made self-containment begin to seem feasible. In Reston, for example, the government has decided to locate a 2,000 man agency.) Moreover, only government could absorb the costs of setting up low-income housing in the towns that wouldn't be an intolerable eye-sore or a potential slum-tract from the very outset—and thus serve to scare off the "better home" buyer. In the well-known Finnish new town, Tapiola, high quality family housing is available for purchase at as low as $2,500—and this with government subsidies. The town is planned to mix such low-cost housing in with homes pricing up to $100,000. But, unlike the American new towns, Tapiola has been built by a non-profit foundation made up of labor unions and welfare organizations.

But even if new towns like Valencia and Foster City could achieve a fairly high degree of self-containment based on employment in their industrial parks, that would not in and of itself make any great contribution to saving our cities. One of the standard criticisms of suburbia is its tendency to select high income groups out of the core city—along with their taxes and purchasing power—and leave behind the poor and less socially adequate, who obviously cannot finance the culture and social services of a major city. It is notorious how crudely suburbia draws on core cities for employment, entertainment, and cosmopolitan glamour . . . but then has downtown merchandise *delivered C.O.D.* so that it will not even have to pay the city's sales tax.

Or let us take a concrete example from the Bay Area that the Foster City developers ought to be forced to face. Early in 1967 a bond issue was defeated in San Francisco which would have provided for some very necessary repairs to the War Memorial Opera House. And more recently still, in August, the Actor's Workshop went out of business after fourteen years of distinguished work, and so San Francisco is left without a major theatrical company. In both cases the explanation is the most stupidly obvious one: money. For a city of 750,000 San Francisco already carries the costs of a fairly good-sized cultural establishment: three major art museums, two opera companies, a symphony orchestra, a ballet company, a major library. . . . And then there is the planetarium, the zoo, the aquarium, the parks, and all the secondary educational-cultural paraphernalia that every major urban center is supposed to provide. Doubtless the money that was needed to support the Workshop and to repair the Opera House is there—in San Francisco—and being put to less worthy uses. But clearly it would be a lot easier to get up these cultural costs if the city could tap the money that is being hoarded up in its well-to-do suburbs.

Is a 35,000 population Foster City going to be able to finance its own repertory theater? The answer is no. Well, is Foster City then going to help San Francisco finance that theater? Again, the answer is no. Foster City's money is ear-marked for barbeque pits, sail boats, shopping on the "flower-splashed mall," and the usual distractions of suburban affluence. But if and when San Francisco does manage to put together the private and public moneys to support another theater company, one can be sure that Foster City (remember it is only twenty convenient minutes from San Francisco) will want to come, see, and enjoy. Just as Foster City will want to be able to send its school children on excursions to San Francisco's art museums, zoo, planetarium, etc.

Valencia will, of course, be some seven times larger than Foster City. But even so: a town of 200,000 is not going to finance an adequate cultural establishment. Indeed, the plans for both Valencia and Foster City couldn't be more vague than they are with respect to the culture of the towns. That is obviously why there is so much hoopla about swimming pools and sauna baths and sailboats. That *is* the "culture" of Valencia and Foster City. And it is as much "culture" as mortgage bankers and land developers are going to worry about providing, which is one great reason why it is ludicrous to talk of these projects as "cities."

Suburbia's selfishness and parasitism has so often been lambasted that it is remarkable to discover how totally unaware of this line of criticism the new town builders are. Lewis Mumford has summed up that criticism by calling the suburb "an asylum for the preservation of illusion." He observes that, historically, suburbia

> was not merely a child-centered environment: it was based on a childish view of the world, in which reality was sacrificed to the pleasure principle. . . . As leisure generally increased, play became the serious business of life; and the golf course, the country club, the swimming pool, and the cocktail party became the frivolous counterfeits of a more varied and significant life.

The Valencia and Foster City developers might almost have decided with a kind of vicious perversity to turn Mumford's criticism into their primary promotional theme. *"Yes,* the golf course and the country club and the swimming pool! What the hell, that's what sells property."

As for the problems of urban blight . . . they have nothing to say. Metropolis decays and starves for money; suburbia rots in imbecilic creature comfort. But they have nothing to say. Here and there a heroic philanthropist struggles to rebuild the life of our cities, or the foundations step in, or, of course, the federal government. But neither the Valencia nor the Foster City developers can claim credit for these city-saving efforts. On the contrary, their work runs in the direction of further destroying the balance between urban needs and suburban affluence and so will do more harm than good. They are continuing to build what Mumford has called the suburban "anti-city."

There are already ominous signs of how far the militant irresponsibility of the new town can go in the direction of cutting itself off from the life and troubles of the metropolis. In some of the "retirement villages" walls and gates have been provided and private police, all to protect the community from the nearby city. The gates close at 9 P.M. and thereafter the police carefully check everybody in and out. I understand from people who have collaborated in planning Valencia that there also the policing problem is one of the matters that is taken most seriously. Long before they worry about symphony orchestras or art museums, the new town builders worry about "how we're going to keep those coons out after dark." The wall, the gate, the watchman: it is like a reversion to the medieval burg. But the medieval town walled *in* the culture of the society. Suburbia walls it *out*.

The quality of American suburban life has been a favorite subject for analysis and complaint for at least two generations now. One can only conclude that the Valencia and Foster City developers—for all they know about physical planning—are scarcely willing to take this critical literature seriously. They talk vaguely in their press releases of the Athenian polis and the Austrian village; they send up empty speculations about the "good city" and the "good life." Valencia, we are told "is dedicated to a concept which is old-fashioned and quietly democratic and decent." A lovely phrase, that. But long before a single resident has moved in, Valencia (like Foster City) has already made room for California's war-related industries. Here again the new towns might be trying to do something to balance out the state's abnormal dependence on war industries. But why struggle with that grave social problem when Lockheed or Motorola stand ready to buy and move in? And so the new towns—our prospective "good cities"—begin their lives with a stake in the arms race and the cold war. What's good for Lockheed is good for Valencia. The political orientation, like the electric range, comes built-in.

It is, finally, when one reaches the issue of politics that Valencia and Foster City prove most lacking. In his *Suburbia: Its People and Their Politics,* Robert C. Wood has concluded that it is very largely the fact or illusion of participative, town-meeting politics that has drawn people from the impersonal cities to the suburb. If that is true, then neither Valencia nor Foster City has cared to pay much attention to Wood. The absolute *last* thing that gets mentioned in their literature is politics, if it gets mentioned at all. One brochure takes up the blessings of Foster City in this order: location, education, shopping, recreation. Period. Some brochures mention incorporation vaguely . . . it will happen later on sometime—after the developers have finished moving in the industrial component, have determined the social and income composition of the town, and have set aside the land and concessions they intend to retain for themselves or their backers. We never discover what the political meaning is of the so-called "villages" and "neighborhoods." Are they really anything but colored areas on a designer's map, ringing the parks and shopping centers?

I suspect the style of home that tends to prevail in these communities gives a hint of how significant the idea of neighborhood is. It is the Eichler home that has perfected what other builders tend to imitate to one degree or another: the house that ingeniously retreats into itself. The garage fronts on the street, shielding the house behind it. One enters and leaves home by car through the garage. The front door is often opened by an electric buzzer and leads into a court, beyond which there is another entrance way. (Finding your way into an Eichler is often a bit of a problem.) The design as a whole focuses on an internal atrium or court. Fences and landscaping close the house in. It is a self-contained unit that holds the family in and retreats from the street, the neighborhood, the world. Not insurmountably to be sure. But the mood of such design is obvious enough. (In the Reston development, however, one should note that homes have been clustered in the midst of collective lawns.)

Now, a city without citizenly participation is a sick city. And if its politics never get beyond selfish defensiveness and an obsessive concern for property values, it is no less sick. It is in fact often one of the diseases of suburbia to be just independent enough to inhibit intelligent regional planning, but much too weak to hold its own against major corporative interests, the military, or even the state highway engineers. In the Bay Area, for example, *all* the communities are far too dependent on military contractors to hold their own politically; but they just manage to frustrate all region-wide efforts to prevent the pell-mell filling-in and contamination of San Francisco Bay.

What do Foster City and Valencia have to say about political life? When and how does the new town take over its own destiny from the developers? On what issues will it have a relevant say so? What will its regional affiliations be? There are no answers to these questions. Apparently because the developers fail to believe that politics really does sell suburbia.

Take a concrete example of what this political vacuousness leads to. New towns like Foster City and Valencia would be ideal places to start up really ambitious consumers' co-operatives. They are large, closed off markets, all of whose major services and merchandising could easily be handled by co-operatives: the groceries, department stores, gas stations, garages, movie houses, etc. And instead of banks, there could be credit unions. The result would be a community that not only saved itself a small fortune by preventing the chain stores from absconding with the profits of its consumption, but one that had some basic control over its economy. And this could lead to a rather interesting ethos—rather like that prevailing among co-operators in the city of Berkeley, California, where consumer co-ops have been stupendously successful. But instead of this option, the developers have of course taken the shortest way to a quick dollar. They have leased to Safeway and Magnin's and Crocker-Anglo Bank, and so they have usurped a basic political decision. Obviously such obtuseness makes it an insane fantasy to speculate upon the chances of setting up *housing* and *producer's* co-operatives as well as consumer co-ops in the developments.

The fact is, one cannot easily imagine what kind of politics will be left when the new towns have been developed. Once the basic decisions have been made and built in, what will the new town governments have to decide—except perhaps the date of the local beauty pageant or whether to rename a few boulevards?

To a certain extent, this building-in of basic decisions seems to be a problem of even government-developed new towns. But it ought not to be beyond the capacity of a government to absorb the costs of patiently experimenting with the problem of taking a prospective new town population into consultation about the shape and character of its town. This could be done in those areas close to major cities which are presently covered with ugly tracts and senseless strip developments. Here, with federal money, state and local governments might begin aggregating already populated land and then planning new town projects *with* the residents, gradually replacing what may already be decaying suburban housing with an organically designed community. In this way new towns might achieve desirable locations close to metropolitan centers as well as democratic involvement in their making. And the latter would be a useful discipline for many of our fair-haired young city-planners whose idea of "what people need" comes out of text books and blueprints and various mystical sources of inspiration. (It is almost comic to hear some of our town planners ambitiously and abstractly brain-storming about "what the suburban house-wife" needs to make life worth living. The answer almost always has to do with the location of things—or perhaps with the putting up of bulletin boards.) Would such land acquisition be expensive? Of course it would. Buying up the land for new towns might almost cost the government as much as it is presently spending *by the month* to devastate Viet Nam—roughly between one and two billion dollars.

The conclusion seems widely accepted now that the privately developed new towns are not going to solve America's urban problems—except for those middle and upper middle class whites who are really in the market for escape rather than a solution. From the look of things, California's new towns are following suit. And in so doing, they are in the way of doing very great harm. For by creating the impression that private enterprise is "carrying the ball" where new towns are concerned, the developers are taking the pressure off the state and the federal government to assume their responsibility in the building of *real* garden cities.

Richard G. Lillard

REVOLUTION BY

INTERNAL COMBUSTION

In California the automobile has collided with civilization. Whatever crushing impact the car has made on life and property in
America, and is making in the world, it is most on display in California, especially in Los Angeles, the type specimen of the auto-
mobile-formed metropolis. "The machine" gained predominance
in California before it reached any such influence anywhere else.
It overwhelmingly won acceptance from a novelty-seeking, easy-
spending, restless population of newcomers in a scenic region of
great distances and in a climate where cars started and ran easily
any day of the year. In California the car first raised on a large
scale new possibilities connected with *Where to live?* and *How to
live? What to do?* and *Where to go to do it?* Statistically the car
is more in evidence here than anywhere else. For better, and for
worse, California is the Number One exhibit of motor vehicle

values, of automobile culture. Far more than the steamship, the railroad, the airplane, or the spaceship, the car here has become *the* symbol of the common man's forward thrust in modern society.

Here, more demonstrably and multitudinously than in any other state or any foreign nation, the car has altered all aspects of life on the earth's surface, in the atmosphere above, and even along the continental shelf, where the state piles up old cars to become havens for sea fishes and mollusks. Like the bomb, the car is a mighty non-human creator of vast problems, such as air pollution, associated with lung diseases, and highway accidents, which maim three persons permanently for every one slaughtered. The car is a leading cause of peacetime death of Californians between the ages of one and thirty-six—before cancer and heart disease take over. It is the only large piece of lethal machinery that a democratic state has allowed eight million amateurs to operate at will under all conditions of terrain, weather, and visibility.

Nowhere outside of California is so high a proportion of the citizenry always on the go, night and day, stepping on the gas in cars and trucks and campers. Nowhere else do so many motorcycles gun and roar along the traffic lanes. Everything has its engine-driven model, including portable county libraries, latrines, congressmen's offices, brothels, blacksmith shops, or confessionals. California leads in the number of people whose legal residence is a mobile home, properly registered as a motor vehicle with four tires and a license plate. Nowhere are drive-in eateries, banks, car-wash places, or motels more numerous. Nowhere else do people so gladly spend on cars. In Los Angeles automotive sales are 18 per cent of all retail sales (compared to 14 per cent in Chicago, 10 per cent in New York). In 1964 the average Los Angeles person spent $1,002 to buy and operate a car (Detroit, second, was $870, New York was $529). Nowhere else are automobile accessories more available, car insurance and car taxes higher—and more taken for granted. In California the motor vehicle is the most-taxed type of personal real property.

Though the bulldozer is reducing landscape to dead level, and sometimes stirring up opposition, the beloved automobile, the *sine qua non* of the masses, has become the popular symbol of modern times, welcome everywhere, provided with room to move and turn and space to rest when immobile, under or in office buildings and dwellings, on roofs, in entire high-rise structures, in forests, on dunes, in gardens. The car is so much a part of the lives of most Californians, children of the century, that they cannot imagine what life would be like if all cars suddenly disappeared. And they dare not face what would then happen to the economy.

California's culture is built not around church or state, sex or money, artistic expression or physical heroism, but around owning and driving the car. Everything gives way to the car and its right-of-way. Parents sacrifice their leisure time to chauffeuring their children to parties and private lessons. Teen-agers commit crimes in order to get gasoline money. High school students must take driver education courses in order to graduate. College students drop out to get jobs and pay for cars they bought to reach the campus in. Divorcées quarrel over who will get the better car. Park commissioners give way to highway commissioners. Architects impair the appearance and functioning of homes and skyscrapers in order to garage cars.

After 1900 the state came more and more to be the world's live specimen of the rubber-tired phase of the industrial revolution. The Tin Lizzie was ending nineteenth-century civilization even before Kaiser Bill finished it off. An early California jester spoke of "automobilitis," just as a recent one has spoken of "autocrazity." For more than sixty years Californians have pioneered in what a UCLA professor calls "automobility." In 1904 and later, the state's two big automobile clubs were the first agencies to begin selecting the best routes west from Missouri and erecting road signs the entire distance. Californians were among the initiators of road racing and track racing, of modern road building, car manufacturing, and of auto club interinsurance exchanges. By 1909 the state had auto rows and auto shows. Before World War I the car was bringing in transcontinental travelers and new settlers, moving migrant farm workers to camps up and down the fertile valleys, taking San Franciscans and Los Angelenos to new subdivisions twice as far out as subdivisions in other states.

Car owners won a hassle with the Secretary of the Interior and in 1913 opened Yosemite Valley to traffic, a fatal victory over scenic sanctity. Cars made their way to Lake Tahoe, through redwood groves, even through individual trees, along seashores, up and down a thousand hills and canyons, taking people into all the countryside as trains had never done. The ordinary family could now travel together, inexpensively, taking the necessities of life along, and camping became a popular activity. More vital than competitors, the car ended cogwheel trains up mountains and slow, casual tourist travel by water—on the Lake Tahoe steamer, the paddlewheel steamboats between San Francisco and Sacramento, and the coastwise liners up the coast from San Diego. The car ended rural isolation in the deserts big as New England states and in mountain towns where dogs had been able to sleep safely at noon in the middle of the main street. The car enabled Los Angeles conqueringly to compete with San Diego for the agricultural produce of Imperial Valley and with Oakland and San Francisco for the produce of the rich southern portion of the San Joaquin Valley.

During the big population booms the car has led to the decline of city centers and of nearby agricultural oases as subdivisions have spread out and begun to jump like chessmen, paving and roofing over the famous California specialty orchard and field crop lands. As the cities have straggled in all directions, including upwards on steep slopes where there are hills, creating a webwork of streets and highways appropriate for movement by automobile, public transportation has died back and often out. Except for San Francisco, largely water-locked, California cities now have no central and peripheral terminuses for rapid transit to run between. The internal combustion engine has exploded metropolis.

The automobile at first improved the small town hotel, since more women were traveling than before, but the motel eventually replaced it, and challenged big city hostelries, too. As a roadside inn with appeal to the self-respecting middle class, the motel first appeared in San Luis Obispo in 1925 with the Milestone Mo-Tel. California and then other western states had motels long before they appeared east of the Missouri River, and the state continues to have the greatest number of them, and also the greatest number of big "motor hotels" with fifty or more units.

By the mid-1920s the power of the car for radical change was more evident here than elsewhere. There were concrete streets and highways, new bridges, straightened and leveled roads, stop signals, white lines, traffic police, traffic courts; there were billboards, big and blatant, stolen-car rings, service stations with "comfort rooms" that gave thousands their first glimpse of modern plumbing; there was a scabby growth of eating places and souvenir stands along highways and of repair shops and auto graveyards near the city limits. The car began to mean litter.

Organizations public and private had new issues: bodily safety, especially at grade crossings, traffic movement on city streets, the gypsy family of migrant workers that camped alongside its car, and the criminal with the means for a fast getaway.

There were new state bureaus to register cars and certificate drivers, to build thoroughfares, and to police highways. Politicians had new issues connected with highway routing, automobile fees, and speed limits. Time after time local ordinances or state laws set precedents for America to follow, for the problems created by an ever-astounding automobile registration called for drastic solutions. While the law did what it could, it could not touch psychological attitudes deep in the heart of most car drivers. Whatever a man's background, however menial, once he is in the driver's seat, and while he remains in it, he is every man's equal.

For members of minority groups, this means not only physical horizontal mobility but also the potential for vertical social mobility.

Statistics help explain the dynamics—and the giantism—of the Californian automobile revolution, for in most automotive tabulations the state leads all other states and all countries except the United States. California leads in the number of registered drivers, more than ten million, including the largest number of women and commercial drivers. It has more licensed drivers than registered voters, more cars than families or houses. Cars multiply faster than families, faster than service stations are opened to take care of them. California leads in registered motor vehicles and trailers, with well over ten million cars in 1966. It leads in the annual number of new car registrations and in the number of used cars sold. During the years 1940-62, while the population grew 146 per cent, car registrations went up 194 per cent and truck registrations 263 per cent. Los Angeles County alone has more cars and trucks than any foreign country. It also has, on the average, fewer persons riding per car than any other American county. The figure is 1.3, which is getting close to the 1.0 ratio of a man to his epidermis. Eighty-five per cent of all Los Angeles families own at least one car (71 per cent in San Francisco and Chicago, 50 per cent in New York). California has more multi-car households than the next two states, Ohio and Texas, combined.

In most automobile figures, the California figure is likely to be one-tenth of the United States figure. But California is ahead of this in registration of the big American cars, for it has around one-sixth of all the Imperials, Lincolns, and Cadillacs in the nation. And it leads by far in imported car outlets. It had 474 such outlets in 1964, when the usual Number Two state, New York, had 363. More than 100,000 foreign cars come through customs in California each year. In Southern California alone, where there were no Volkswagens in 1947, there are now 230,000. On some Hollywood side streets three or four Volkswagens at once will sometimes be the only cars in sight. The Culver City distributor, whose territory is Southern California and southern Nevada, Arizona, and Hawaii, now sells around 30,000 a year.

California leads in the size and effectiveness of automobile organizations. The Automobile Club of Southern California, with 711,000 master members, is the largest automobile club on earth. The northern twin, California State Automobile Association, with more than 522,000 master members, operates all over Nevada. Together the two associations make up 16 per cent of the membership of the American Automobile Association in the United States and Canada.

Dozens of freeway intersections, notably in San Francisco, Oakland, and the seventy-six Los Angeles County cities, carry 100,000 cars or more on an average day. A one-mile stretch on the Santa Monica Freeway in central Los Angeles now carries on the daily average 219,000 cars, mostly of commuters. For many natives, as for visitors, heavy traffic creates an exciting scene to gasp at. Hillside hosts place their cocktail guests so that they can gaze at the lights of choked traffic on the freeways in the valley below.

California cars are a potent factor in making tourism a leading industry in western states and the leading one in Nevada. Most of the millions who visit the eastern shore of Lake Tahoe, Reno, or Las Vegas come by car, and 60 per cent of these are from California. Indeed, of the drivers whose destination is Nevada, 75 per cent are from California. Before the era of good roads and automobiles, Nevada was California's colony; the California car and Nevada gambling and showmanship have now in a way reversed the relationship.

Despite the labors of local and national safety councils, California has long been the national leader in the absolute number of deaths caused by motor cars. There were 4,318 in 1963, out of 43,600 in the country.[1]

---

[1] Relatively, however, in the number of deaths per 100 million motor-vehicle miles, it is in the middle group of states.

Although California does not assemble cars and trucks as massively as do Michigan and several other states, it is a special and radical force in the testing and designing of cars, inside and out. In the era of Barney Oldfield, when cars were becoming popular sports machines, as during the Vanderbilt Cup races in San Francisco and Santa Monica, or during the formidable road races across raw deserts between San Diego or Los Angeles and Phoenix, years before rivers were bridged for motor traffic, California racers devised improvements in knee-action, spark plugs, radiators, tires, or streamlining. In 1917 a writer called Southern California "an incubating ground for automobile inventors" and "a coming automobile accessory manufacturing site," and thousands of items since have sustained the prediction.

In the 1930s came California innovations in drag racing, notably on dry desert lakebeds, where men and women roared in "lakesters" at speeds up to 150 miles per hour. There was the rise, centered in Los Angeles, of the hot-rod car, the National Hot Rod Association, hot-rod publications, and hot-rod manufacturers. Amateurs and professionals alike dropped front axles, lowered springs and frames in the center, souped up engines, worked on axial flow superchargers, fuel mixtures, and fuel injections. In 1945 by one estimate there were 3,000 hot rodders in the world, almost all of them in Southern California; now there are converts all over America. Southern California also produced the Offenhauser engines, long famous as winners at Indianapolis, and the celebrated Iskenderian racing and drag camshafts, with their delicate, special grinds on the lobes, designed for exquisite timing. Nowadays the annual Grand Prix at Riverside attracts 50,000 racing fans to watch heroes such as Parnelli Jones.

The racers are part of the busy California sub-world of car addicts. Teen-agers and also movie and television stars, and other archons of automotive fashions, patronize kustom-kar shops, admired by insiders, like those of Ed Roth, Bill Cushenbery, or George Barris. Such men have devised things later taken up by

Detroit, such as tailfins, bubbletops, low-slung bodies, bucket seats, exhaust pipes coming through the rear bumper, movable twin headlights, and bizarre paint jobs. Tom Wolfe takes up this eccentric fringe of the automobile industry in his *Kandy-Kolored Tangerine-Flake Streamline Baby*. There is extra enthusiasm and money in California for road rallies, special automotive shows, antique car collecting, and automobiliana of all sorts. The "auto-rotic" implications of this are suggested by the TV program *My Mother the Car*.

California climate and inclination, California demand and sales, fathered outdoor living vehicles, now bought and used everywhere—the trailer, the camper, the enormous mobile home, the station wagon, and the rover-type machines that go up mountain sides or sand dunes or over marshy ground. California has also fathered or spurred the development of sports cars, convertibles, roadsters, compacts, whatever, made by old-line companies but given light-headed new names such as Sting Ray, Malibu, Mustang, Catalina, Avanti, or Toronado. At the Detroit auto show a few years back an executive said that California-inspired design "has put excitement back into the automobile . . . Moods start in California, then sweep across the country."

It was California and Florida before World War I that saw the first small start in truck and public bus lines. Except in San Francisco, buses have since exterminated streetcars, trucks have forced the railroads, for survival, to enter the trucking business and to play piggyback, and California is easily truck state Number One. The state has a million and one-half trucks, several hundred thousand more than does oily Texas, twice as many as either Pennsylvania or New York. Each year it registers 12 per cent of all the nation's new trucks and trailers.

Trucks dominate the roadway through much of the state's scenery. U.S. 99, from Los Angeles over the rugged Tehachapi Mountains to Bakersfield and Fresno, is the busiest truck route in the world, with trucks in motion lining up like blocks of one-story buildings. Other heavy truck routes are U.S. 99 between Imperial Valley and Los Angeles; stretches of U.S. 101 between San Diego and San Francisco; and the main routes eastward: U.S. 40 between San Francisco and Reno and U.S. 60 between Indio and Blythe and Phoenix. Like cars, trucks, whether large or small, are everywhere. Public utilities and retail giants have big fleets, and common carriers for hire transport almost 90 per cent of all goods moved in the state, leaving little for trains and a tiny fraction for boats. Nearly every product grown in California, the premier agricultural state, is at one time or another on a truck. Many crops harvested one day are 500 miles away the next morning in an air-conditioned truck. Three-fifths of all California communities get their freight only by truck. The new city of Lakewood, 70,000 persons in 1963, was totally constructed by motor transport and remains totally served by the same, and nearby Long Beach, 375,500 persons (plus visiting beauty queens), has had no passenger train service since 1932, no interurban service since 1961. It lives by the truck, as by the car and bus.

Demobilization sent back doughboys taught to drive trucks, and after pneumatic truck tires came in, and bigger, faster rigs, the industry began its growth. In 1930 California had a truck for every 57 persons; in 1964 it had a truck for every 14. At making mechanical innovations, Californians early took the lead in the West, and westerners took the lead in America. Mechanics and engineers developed arrangements of axles and tires that spread enormous weights evenly over road surfaces, and they made a thousand improvements in engines, chassis, couplings, refrigeration, brakes, and safety devices. Truckers learned how to tie down the trunks of coast redwoods and Sierra sugar pines, towering loads of baled alfalfa hay, and slippery piles of lumber. Western Highway Institute, California Trucking Association, and other organizations lobbied for laws allowing changes. The 13½-foot height and the 65-foot overall length became legal in California and the West before they did farther east. The same is true of the most important new development, flexible and economical, called "doubles operation." This means a tractor, two semitrailers, and a converter dolly. "Doubles" were legal and successful here long before they began to be accepted in the Mississippi Valley. John B. Springer, trucking association official in San Francisco, was a force behind this pathbreaking development, which has spread to France, where the semitrailers are called twins, *jumeaux,* and where Springer has been toasted as *le père des jumeaux français.*

The rise of motor hauling has been one more pressure on California educators to further bypass the liberal arts and favor vocational training. California leads the states in the number of institutions that offer motor-vehicle transportation courses and majors, from universities giving the Ph.D. to junior colleges giving the A.A. degree.

Though public and private planners are more active in California than in most other states, they have not known what to do about the automobile other than to accept it. They cannot indict a mechanism that is the alter ego of most voters. The result is that in old-established cities like Oakland and Nevada City, Pasadena, and Los Angeles, public planners have at most directed the retreat of civilization in the face of the all-conquering vehicle.

The automobile's needs have led men to smash out, as if by bombing, great raw spaces in downtown areas. In many cities two-thirds of the downtown is devoted to cars in some way, including service stations and used-car lots, and two-thirds, too, of all sales space. New suburban stores allow three-fourths of their acreage to cars, and discount store officials foresee five-sixths or even six-sevenths for cars.

Having choked the cities and partially destroyed them, the automobile has carried the escaping populace to the agricultural or wilderness periphery, where subdividers, blessed by county supervisors, have turned ranches and recreational open space into shopping districts and towns for vets with kids, or millionaires, or college people, or self-zoned industrialists, or "senior citizens." There are big new residential cities like Fremont near San Jose, El Dorado Hills planned for 75,000 in twelve villages east of Sacramento, or University City near the new branch of the state university in the La Jolla district of San Diego. There are new recreational cities in the far-flung deserts and at the southern end of sky-high Lake Tahoe.

To make way for the automobile and the truck—not for people—California planners have widened streets and highways, cutting down handsome trees, spoiling residential ambience, demolishing buildings that are the tangible proof of history, cutting like a mowing machine through millennial redwood groves and like a quarrying saw through the immemorial glacial polish of High Sierra lakeshores. Roadmakers have displaced foothill creeks and smothered Pacific shore lagoons.

Fifty years ago California was the first state to set up a statewide system of highways. In 1957 it was the first to set up a statewide system of freeways. Three years ago it adopted a 5,500-mile scenic highway system that involved restricting outdoor ads, preserving scenery intact in roadside corridors, and guarding agricultural lands by not cutting through them. This radical *mea culpa,* half a century late, might rescue souvenir fragments of California the Golden. For state tradition was the other way. Freeways have smashed like the *Wehrmacht*[2] through the centers of cities, particularly in modest or low-rent areas, though at present San Francisco and a few other self-respecting cities are trying to fight off freeways or get them out of sight, sound, and smell. In general, freeway values are automotive values and win easy victories, and interchanges are the public monuments of triumph. The intersection of the Santa Monica and the San Diego

---

[2] One must remember that the argument for the present U. S. interstate highway system, signed into law by General Eisenhower, was a military one. These are roads for "defense."

freeways, a three-level interchange that is a high-flying kind of mobile sculpture, incorporates thirty traffic lanes and occupies ninety acres of land.

Officials now propose to pave over unique wine-producing soil in the Napa Valley in order to supplement a charming country road and expedite the movement of cars, and they propose to bridge the entrance to Emerald Bay on Lake Tahoe, spoiling one of the remaining untouched vistas on that indigo-blue lake, once famed for pure water, now turning green at the edges where run-off sewage from gambler-autoists supports a booming population of algae.

Although most planners abdicate to the vehicle, foreseeing no substitute for it, a few, like Victor Gruen of Beverly Hills and Vienna, work to counteract it, to tame it, to fortify the city against it by designing street plans that keep the cars away, by burying traffic alive underground or by building shopping malls. The California Pedestrian Mall Law of 1960, permissive and radical, said that there is a need in certain areas "to separate pedestrian travel from vehicular travel . . . to protect the public safety or otherwise to serve the public interest and convenience." Already Fresno, Pomona, and several other cities are experimenting with malls which, at most, make motor vehicles taboo in certain places at certain times.

Most colleges and universities, accepting the students' cars, have bulldozed away campus amenities to make way for them, and have even made money by charging parking fees. But the pioneering chancellor, of the University of California at Santa Cruz, D. H. McHenry, discourages resident students from bringing cars to the campus. In 1966, 85 per cent of the students were without cars, and a year later housing preference came to students free from the distraction of cars. McHenry observes that young people who work nights and weekends in order to support cars are not likely to read as they should, nor do they participate in campus life. "If everybody has his own wheels, the quorum tends to melt."

The Santa Cruz attempt to make education peripatetic again points up one great loss to civilization in California, the loss of the habit and pleasure of walking. The pedestrian, around whom all civilization centered until the automotive era, disappeared in California after cities began to roll outward on rubber tires. Foot-walkers are so rare now as to be suspicious characters in exclusive residential areas. Strolling, popular as recently as fifty years ago, is so obsolescent that new streets in hillside tracts provide no sidewalks at all. Despite the growth in population, hiking has died back in the auto-infested mountains. The Park Service that has paved Yosemite and Kings Canyon meadows for parking has been able drastically to reduce the mileage of high trails it needs to maintain, for lack of use. Even window shopping, once passion-ate activity of an acquisitive society, has seriously declined, ex-cept in downtown San Francisco, although some people now window shop from their cars at red signals. The common thing is to park under the department store and to escalate directly into the building, like miners, or to park on the blacktop surface behind the store and enter it from the rear, like employees.

The California driver, in shoes that never need resoling, races like an astronaut amid a ton or two of metal, generally all alone, from one specialized stop to another, with his route mapped out in his head. He is more isolated from conversation, or from re-laxed personal meditation, than a solitary horseman in Mongolia or a hermit on Mount Athos. He is deprived of flirtation, alcohol, or television. He is self-incarcerated in a glassed-in, flammable cell. Often he thus encases himself daily for two hours of com-muting. Sometimes on a pleasure weekend, when he is between home and beach or desert or mountain, he may sit for hours, an unwilling captive, during a freeway tie-up as long as twenty-five miles, owing to an accident or some roadwork. Never were more persons who are a few feet apart less sociable and less aware of each other than are the drivers of the 343,000 cars that use the 4-level freeway interchange in Los Angeles any average 24-hour day.

As people cease to walk, accepting poor circulation and heart trouble as substitutes, athletes are in poorer condition. Says one college coach, "It's hard to get their legs in shape because of too much riding in cars or spectator sports." People seeking recreation are no more expected to walk to get to their destination than they are when they get there. Men hunt in jeeps and fish from scooters. They climb peaks by means of gasoline power. The 2-volume *California Outdoor Recreation Plan* of 1960 hinged on a set of 1958 figures showing that one-day round-trip pleasure jaunts in California automobiles came to 24 billion miles for the year.

The car has been a potent force in the growth of California to pre-eminence in population, per capita wealth, modern luxury, and glamour. It has helped make California a new wonder of the world. But it has also made California Number One in automobile noise, as in traffic congestion and highway death. "Acoustic pollution" has spoiled hundreds of miles of residential streets. *Go— Transport Times of the West* calls truck engine and exhaust noise "one of the most complex problems of our modern times." More than any other one source the car is the cause of the celebrated California smog, another problem as complex as petroleum, the gasoline engine, sunshine, weather, and human nature combined. The fight against smog has produced unprecedented public agencies. The creation of the Los Angeles County Air Pollution Control District and then of the State Motor Vehicle Pollution Control Board has led to startling but long overdue invasions of private enterprise and private irresponsibility. Public regulation has been a great gain for the public good.

There are people who see the car as revolutionary in the evil sense of destruction—destruction of city and country and wilderness, of established human values. After opening up the landscape the car is becoming the only thing in sight. The glitter of chrome, the odor of exhaust and crankcase fumes, the clamor of engines and the shriek of brakes, the slamming of car doors and the squeals and thuds of collisions, the sting of smog in the eyes and the gasp for air in the bronchial tubes—these are upon the land. The driver is a dupe.

In contrast there are those who see the car as an undisguised blessing, as revolutionary in the sense of providing a new and valuable tool, an adaptable and efficient mechanical assistant to men as they work, travel, progress, and happily live out their days. The driver is king.

Both sides agree that in California the motor vehicle has been a mighty force for alteration. All agree that nowhere else on earth is it so thoroughly integrated into human society. Here is the place to study the future of other areas where the car is just now spreading to the masses, for California prodigiously shows mankind how transportation by means of motor vehicles can become an end in itself. The car accelerates change, rerouting civilization, and the frightened driver, strapped to his vehicle, must go where the white lines lead him.

Samuel E. Wood

THE FREEWAY REVOLT
AND WHAT IT MEANS

The California revolt against freeways started with a simmering of protest from cities in the hot San Joaquin Valley in the early 1950s. It reached a rolling boil in 1967 when San Francisco refused 180 million "free" dollars' worth of freeways in order to protect its parks and neighborhoods from destruction or disfigurement. Five or six years ago the freeway revolt was isolated in a few communities. Today it is a general condition, and the major battles, which will be fought in the legislature, are yet to be joined.

As construction moves ahead on 12,400 miles of California's freeway system, scores of citizens' organizations are today battling the Division of Highways and often their own elected local governments on projected freeway plans. From San Diego to Eureka citizens are in effect standing before the bulldozers to prevent the destruction of parks and open space, streams and bay shores, hill tops and canyons. In most cases *ad hoc* efforts have been little and too late. All too often the public has been aroused only to find that critical decisions had already been made. In every case, the destructive projects which generated fiery opposition had the approval of local government. Sacramento, for example, *asked for* the freeway which cut off the city from its waterfront and destroyed dozens of historic buildings.

Pitched battles to save community values are now being fought at Santa Barbara, Laguna Beach, Malibu, Beverly Hills, South Pasadena, Ladera Heights, Newport Beach, San Francisco, and San Diego. Confrontations between citizens' groups and the Division of Highways over the invasion of park and open space land and the destruction of amenities have occurred at Lake Tahoe, the north coast redwood areas of California, and the Napa Valley.

In spite of the revolt, Californians' love for the automobile has made their state the most motor-vehicle dependent in the Union. By 1980 there will probably be more trucks and automobiles registered than it has people today. But love for the private auto is matched by a seeming hate for the very freeways which promise to make auto travel quicker, safer, and less nerve wracking. This ambivalence results not alone from hatred of freeways *per se* (which no doubt does exist), but from a general alarm over the entire process of freeway development.

The California freeway revolt has reached the stage where policies and procedures of the monolithic and politically protected Division of Highways and the Highway Commission are now under sharp attack. There is a growing awareness that until these policies and procedures are brought under a more democratic control, the division will continue on its own adventures, largely unresponsive to the citizenry.

The division employs almost 17,000 people and runs on a yearly budget that ranges close to $800 million dollars a year. Since it is sustained by a constitutionally protected gasoline tax, the division is free from the close review of program and performance that comes to other state agencies from the budget making and review process of the governor's office and the legislature. Supervision of the division comes from a rubber-stamp commission, a prisoner of the division, on which it is completely dependent for advice on both technical and policy matters.

One of the major reasons for public disaffection is the division's obvious lack of concern for what its freeways do to the beauty and productivity of the state.

California highways, according to the division, are "planned and located to provide the maximum service to highway users, . . . and to improve the economic and general welfare of the community." The division claims that this method of location insures the greatest possible return for the money invested. Lip service is given to the "economic and general welfare of the community" but great emphasis in route selection is placed on a "user benefit" formula which presumably gives the greatest dollar savings to highway users.

In the process, however, other economic, social, and esthetic effects of freeway location receive little attention. It may be true that the primary beneficiary is the highway user, but this user is also a human being who is often interested in more than saving a few pennies a day or a few minutes on the freeway. He is also interested in maintaining the quality and stability of his city's neighborhoods; he wants his local parks and historic structures left untouched. The attack on state parks, beginning with the north coast redwoods, has pained him. The outcry led Governor Pat Brown to postpone the division's plans that would have bridged the mouth of Lake Tahoe's Emerald Bay and slashed through the giant redwoods of Perry Creek Park.

But the victories in the countryside remain few; in the next ten years the division plans to occupy 1,000 acres of California's parks. This destruction will permit a savings of about twelve miles out of the total 12,400 miles.

In the cities, the division, in its mission to solve urban transportation problems with freeways alone, has shown a penchant for messing up well-conceived local plans. It located freeways contrary to adopted city plans in Glendale, Fremont, Pasadena, and Santa Barbara. It proposes to destroy the most beautiful section of Pomona, to wreck the charm and quality of Beverly Hills, and to destroy the waterfront and way of living of the people of Newport Beach, in spite of a cheaper alternate route. Freeways have clipped seven acres out of the beautiful campus of Mills College, disrupted land development plans at the University of California at Davis, and displaced the Home for the Blind in Oakland. Parks in Oakland, Sacramento, Chico, Los Angeles, and San Diego, among others, have been scarred by the division's bulldozers.

The division thinks big, and its most ambitious proposal to date and at the same time perhaps the crowning example of blindness to other values is its joint plan with the Bureau of Public Roads to use three atomic blasts to knock down Clark Mountain on Interstate 15 between the towns of Baker and Las Vegas. Currently, this stretch of highway is a four-lane divided highspeed freeway recently constructed. If Clark Mountain were blown off the map the highway men could get a straight line and probably cut off two miles and two minutes in driving speed. The Atomic Energy Commission is interested, of course, in blasting the mountain as an experiment in the peaceful uses of atomic energy. Similar preliminary investigations have been made by the division to blast a 320-foot-deep hole for eight lanes of freeway through the Bristol Mountains between Barstow and Needles. Both of these enterprises—if atomic energy costs nothing and we were willing to abrogate the Test Ban Treaty—would save the freeway constructors several millions of dollars.

The workings of the Division of Highways are fascinating to behold. Even major cities of California, San Francisco for example, find difficulty in meeting the array of tactics and political and financial power brought to bear against them.

Communities are off-balance with the division from the time the first line is drawn by draftsmen and countersigned by an engineer. This line, and others for alternate routes, are cleared with the local chamber of commerce which in turn provides "local support." A staff of highway district representatives works with its city and county counterparts to convince elected officials that the division's chosen route is the most advantageous. These local bits and pieces are assembled into a statewide program and defended by the State Chamber of Commerce and its local units in hearings before the State Highway Commission.

Encirclement has been, and is still, a major tactic of the Division, as illustrated by current struggles in El Monte, Chico, El Cajon, Santa Barbara, and South Pasadena. This gambit calls for freeway location and construction, if necessary, to a reluctant city's limits, thereby infecting all the property on the proposed route with freeway blight. Land in the right-of-way can't be sold, rented, or even improved. Traffic draining off both ends floods city streets. The only defense local government has against the highway men is its right to refuse to sign an agreement for the closure of streets and roads. Once the division's preferred location is made known, the economic interests waiting for payment under condemnation and for construction generate pressure for the acceptance of the location.

Actual acquisition of property along the route has proceeded during the process of these negotiations. This happened in San Bruno. The city refused to accept the division's location, but the division nonetheless purchased property along the right-of-way, confident that in the long run the community would "be negotiated" out of its refusal, and that the division eventually would have its way. This practice was specifically prohibited in 1967 by the legislature.

A tactic even more frequently used is that of divide and conquer. In Sacramento, to illustrate one manipulation, the division submitted plans for small segments of the total alignment piecemeal to small groups within the metropolitan area. By doing this the total impact of the entire freeway could not be seen by all those affected. The opposition which might have been generated against the total freeway plan never materialized.

Another method the division uses to divide and conquer is to propose a great number of alternate routes, as it did in Palo Alto and Pasadena, for example, which adversely affect many local inhabitants, thus throwing neighborhoods into mortal conflict with each other. In the process, the division, like Solomon of old, can look down on the squabbling natives and choose the route of its own pleasure, sure in the knowledge its choice will please the majority of the confused.

If all other tactics fail, the division can call on the historic ally of all bureaucracies—time. Elected officials come and go, some with and some without the support of the district engineers and their allies, the local chambers of commerce. In any case the division can afford to wait while its employees "pass the word" that the freeway will be lost forever—that the funds will be allocated to a more co-operative community. Time finally gained the support of the Los Angeles County Board of Supervisors in the two-year effort to enlarge the four-lane freeway through La Canada Valley to eight. And so the process continues, but not without a slight shift toward more effective public control.

In 1965, the State Assembly Committee on Natural Resources, Planning and Public Works published a review of public efforts to make the highway planning process more responsive to total public interest. The study showed that the commission is still dominated by the division, that it still constructs freeways in a single-purpose, heavy-handed fashion, and that it largely neglects community needs, park and recreation values and esthetic factors. During the past three years, the division and its supporters were able to defeat proposals that would furnish the commission with an independent staff; closely regulate location procedures to protect community and esthetic values and prevent the single-purpose occupation of public parks by highways and freeways. Most important, a recent effort to develop a statewide multi-modal transportation system related to state development objectives and an agency to administer this plan was killed in conference committee after passing both houses of the legislature.

But thanks in good part to the thousands of citizen dollars and millions of hours of voluntary effort spent in California's freeway revolt, some small cracks have appeared in the monolithic structure controlling transportation in California. Several minor but nevertheless significant reform measures have been passed during the last three years. No longer can the division lean on the legal section providing that highways must be constructed in the most "direct and practical" locations. The administrator of the transportation agency is no longer ex officio chairman of the Highway Commission. Hearings may become more sympathetic to local protest now that they are conducted by independent officers rather than Division of Highways personnel. The Highway Commission must at least give an *ex post facto* justification for each route which must show that community values as well as user benefits are considered. And for the first time, sketches and models of all proposals and alternates must be submitted at hearings if requested by local government.

Community revolts have resulted in some large and a number of small victories—all at the local level. A united community of Novato convinced the Highway Commission that the division-endorsed freeway down the middle of the city was a poor location. The commission reversed its field twice before agreeing with the city of Fremont that the civic center and its park was not the place for a freeway. El Cajon won a compromise location that fits into its general plan. While the beauty of Monterey Peninsula took a beating when a freeway cut and gouged Carmel Hill, it won a battle when the "can of worms" interchange was reluctantly surrendered by the division, and Monterey's historic Customs House, First Theater, Pacific House, and Casa del Oro were saved from a freeway location by a grant of $43 million from the Urban Renewal Administration. Aroused neighborhood groups were so strong at Long Beach that the city council refused to accept any crosstown freeway whatsoever and ordered the Planning Commission to eliminate it from the master plan.

San Francisco has fought the Division of Highways to an absolute standstill. It would appear to be a victory. The city could remain strong and determined in its revolt but I doubt that even San Francisco can hold out against the raw power of the division and the commission forever.

The fact is the division is in fine shape to bargain with the city. Some freeways the city wants, but may not get; other freeways it doesn't want, but may have forced upon it. The division still wants to construct a freeway that threatens the watershed of one of San Francisco's reservoirs. The division favors a new Bay crossing that will increase congestion and take more through traffic into San Francisco's downtown area; it favors the completion of the Embarcadero Freeway.

On the other hand, the city wants the immediate widening of the Golden Gate Bridge approaches as part of the Interstate System; wants an immediate crossing that will rescue the downtown area from additional congestion and loss of land, and desires a more acceptable solution to the Embarcadero Freeway.

In spite of legislative effort to knock down the defacing Embarcadero Freeway, the stub-end still waits to be joined with the network when the citizens' opposition weakens and new members are elected to the Board of Supervisors. Already the 180 millions of interstate dollars earmarked for the construction of Golden Gate and Pan Handle freeways is being transferred to Southern California for the Century freeway. Thus San Francisco is being deprived of interstate funds because it stood firmly against the State Division of Highways. It is claimed that the San Francisco success also stiffened the revolt of Ladera Heights, which produced an Assembly request that called a halt to further work on the route.

California Going, Going . . . , written by Alfred E. Heller and this writer and published by "California Tomorrow" in 1962, contained the first general indictment of the havoc wrought by the Division of Highways on the state's beauty and productivity. The study evoked an outraged response from the division, printed at an estimated public cost of about three times the original study. Both documents gave credence to the existence of a widespread revolt and helped form a bond between revolters.

In 1963 several citizen groups joined hands to create the state-wide California Citizens Freeway Association, which during the two years of its existence extended help with a fair amount of success to fourteen embattled localities. But local freeway victories will not win the war, and in 1965 citizen organizations throughout the state assisted in creating the Planning and Conservation League for Legislative Action, to backstop legislative and administrative programs to maintain and enhance California's beauty and productivity. The paid lobbyist of the league and its friends in Sacramento fought for the passage of highway, parkway, and beautification bills. For the first time citizen revolt organizations are able to focus on basic statewide freeway reform measures.

At a minimum, reforms must include creation of a full-fledged state transportation agency, able to encourage statewide and regional transportation systems, under the policy direction of a reconstituted transportation commission. The umbrella of the new agency could cover highways, air fields, maritime shipping, rapid transit, and railroads. Metropolitan areas must have more control over the systems they are now planning, with access to state and federal gas tax money to develop and manage systems tailored to local requirements. The normal budget review characteristic of California government needs to be restored to the transportation sector. Gas tax revenues could be used to finance public transit. As long as the state and federal gas tax money is held sacrosanct from use by rapid transit and integrated mass transit systems, congestion in metropolitan areas will increase in spite of accelerated freeway construction. The spillover of benefits to the freeway user from all forms of mass transit that reduce the number of cars on a freeway during peak hours is obvious.

Except for a few notable examples such as North American Aviation's "California's Integrated Transportation Study," most transportation planning is stuck in the nineteenth century. The North American study could be a prototype for the imaginative planning needed to develop advanced systems of mass transportation. Systems analysis used for weaponry and space exploration could also be used to produce new modes with more speed and safety and new methods of underground tunneling that would protect surface space and amenities.

The California Division of Highways is already anticipating a second federal bonanza, a post-1972 highway construction program. If the state doesn't want freeways only as a solution to our transportation needs, massive efforts, first for research and development and then for construction, equal perhaps in cost to our moon probe efforts, will be required.

If the California revolt proves anything, it proves again that the motor vehicle is no longer an acceptable single solution for the movement of people and goods, but it demonstrates more.

The fact is that Emerald Bay has not been bridged nor Golden Gate Park invaded. This certainly is not because the Bureau of Public Roads has been able to restrain the powerful California highway men; it may be because the freeway revolt of neighborhood groups became a statewide force and in the process gained support of local government and placed increasing pressure on the legislature and the governor himself.

Jennifer Cross

AMERICA'S LABORATORY
FOR SOCIAL CHANGE

California in the sixties is the pacemaker in the struggle against poverty, crime, addiction, aging, and the more recent dislocation of family ties in our rich, complex, and shifting way of life. In many ways, she leads out of necessity. For, while becoming America's richest and fastest-growing state, she has developed ominous social blight; poverty, urban and rural slums, the highest crime rate, and the second highest addiction and divorce rates in the country. Fortunately, California has always shown a remarkable ability to cope with her problems, displaying a social inventiveness which has been the pattern for other states. Californians tend to believe that what they do today America does tomorrow, and, in many respects, this is true.

Given the simmering situations in Watts and Oakland, California does not deserve more than a "C" average for coping with poverty. Yet in some areas she is doing excellent pioneering work, which will certainly be taken up elsewhere. For example, the new careers concept—formulated by Pearl and Reissman in their book *New Careers for the Poor,* based on trial projects in New York, Chicago, Philadelphia, and Pittsburgh—is being developed in a way that may well get it off the ground as the most sensible and dignified solution for chronic poverty and technological unemployment.

Briefly, its proponents believe that new careers should provide the poor with meaningful work, which will make them feel useful, and an automation-proof opportunity, with on-the-job training, allowing a gradual progress from unskilled to professional status. Such careers are to come chiefly from the fast-growing public sector, particularly at state, city, and county levels, in education, health, and welfare departments. Here, addition to and reapportionment of existing professional jobs would swell much needed human services, provide work for the poor, and allow them to use their special ability to communicate with their own kind as teachers' aides, health aides, counselors, homemakers, and neighborhood workers.

California's contribution is unusual in that it occurs in a difficult and controversial sphere—corrections—and provides the nearest thing yet to a workable training model. In January, 1964, J. Douglas Grant, then at the California Medical Facility, Vacaville, started a two-year project funded by the National Institute of Mental Health to train twenty-four inmates in what could be called the practical philosophy of new careers. Instead of merely being teachers' aides or neighborhood workers, they were to go into the community and create such jobs for other people. They called themselves change agents.

At first sight the project did not look promising. All the students had dubious records, and Grant had to develop a training program from scratch. On the bright side, all were young, enthusiastic, and fairly intelligent, with an eleventh-grade education, at least four months in a therapeutic community (the ICE program), and all were considered by staff and peer group to have a reasonable chance of early and successful parole.

They learned as they went along. In an intensive eight-month course, half in prison, half outside, they learned basic skills at a workable level—interviewing, research methods, writing, administrative procedure, plus an outline of organizational change, group dynamics, and social trends and issues. More important, they learned how to learn about their own strengths and weaknesses and how to work as a team. They worked hard, rarely less than twelve hours a day and sometimes sixteen, letting off steam (and dropping their veneer of intellectual jargon) in regular group therapy sessions.

Eighteen months later thay had enough collective insight to formulate a set of learning principles specially geared to people who are in a hurry but without formal education, producing the theory of a curriculum which is practical, flexible, and quite unacademic.

Now they have been seeded throughout California to pass on what they have learned and to create new careers for the poor. The main center of activity is at the New Careers Development Organization, Oakland, a non-profit firm headed by J. Douglas Grant, and staffed by a number of the boys from inside, which is primarily helping to administer the one-sixth of the city of Oakland's five-million-dollar job development program which is devoted to new careers. Elsewhere the old new-careers people, and a new generation of graduates (many of them ex-offenders) are working with the California Department of Corrections, particularly the probation department and the youth authority. In Los Angeles, an enterprising ex-con has teamed up with some motion picture people to start making new-careers training films. And in Sacramento there is a move to put a small group of ex-offenders on the legislators' research staff by summer 1968 to work on federal funding for the new careers programs.

Outside the state, the Vacaville people are in New York City, working with the human resources administration, in the New York state division of youth. They are in the state of Washington, where the governor has budgeted $200,000 for new careers development and promises civil service positions by 1969. They are in Trenton, New Jersey, and east St. Louis. Most important, perhaps, they are in Washington, D.C., trying to prevent crime legislation from degenerating into mere riot control. One of Mr. Grant's boys, Larry Dye, is on the research staff of the Joint Commission on Correctional Manpower and Training, working with academic sociologists throughout the country on a two-million-dollar study of the role of the offender as a resource person in the whole administration of justice.

Four years after starting their new life, the Vacaville people are making from $7,000–$15,000 a year (average $9,000). All but one have gone straight . . . while half their matching control group of twenty-five are back inside, a reminder that Satan has a harder job finding mischief for hands which are actively and honorably employed.

California is also tackling poverty problems on experimental lines, using some state money plus what new career graduates, somewhat disparagingly, call "soft money," i.e., anti-poverty and other federal funds.

At the end of 1966 thirteen multi-service centers were set up in areas with a critical poverty problem—south central and east Los Angeles, Venice, Long Beach, San Diego, San Bernardino, Bakersfield, Fresno, Stockton, San Francisco, Oakland, Richmond, and Vallejo. Here, low income people can get the full range of state services under one roof—which is not only a great practical convenience to those who often do not have cars, but a way to help overcome the ignorance and intimidation which prevent the poor from taking full advantage of social services.

One of the newest and most experimental services being offered is consumer information and education—not, of course, new in themselves but new in being one of the first concerted, large scale efforts to cater to low income people. Despite the growing realization that the poor do pay more, existing consumer organizations and the consumer protection activities of federal agencies nearly all serve the middle class. They neither deal with the specific problems of the poor, nor speak their language and therefore fail to reach them. Mrs. Helen Nelson, lately California's Consumer Counsel, has been trying to do both through the multi-service centers. Here she was able to draw on the experience of several groups throughout the state which are working in this branch of consumer education. Biggest of these is BAND (Bay Area Neighborhood Development Foundation), a three-year-old demonstration project in Oakland and San Francisco, which runs three service centers, three credit unions, a consumer action council, and has organized consumer workshops and fairs, and produced simply written literature in English and Spanish.

While these programs mostly affect low income city dwellers, efforts are also being made to help their rural opposite numbers. One experiment is a $1,300,000 legal services program, first funded by the OEO in July, 1966, and the first of its kind in the country to be run for low income people in rural areas. Working from a Los Angeles headquarters and ten regional offices, the executive organization, California Rural Legal Assistance, is teaching the poor about their legal rights, providing them with legal advice, and representing them at court.

During 1967 CRLA proved its mettle in two precedent-setting class actions, to the discomfiture of both Governor Reagan and U.S. Secretary of Labor, W. Willard Wirtz. In the first, CRLA backed a recipient of Medi-Cal to challenge the legality of a new set of regulations abolishing 295 million dollars' worth of benefits available to the medically indigent, which Governor Reagan had proposed as part of his economy drive. CRLA won, and the regulations were nipped in the bud. They also won a case brought by a group of California farm workers compelling the Secretary of

Labor to enforce 8 US Code 1182 (a) (14) barring the use of *braceros,* whom, they feared, might be re-employed by local growers to undercut their own meager wages, and break down their attempts to unionize.

Millions of dollars in federal money has also been pumped in since the early 1960s to boost California's three migrant help programs. In the first serious official attempt to alleviate "Grapes of Wrath" conditions among itinerant farm workers since the 1930s, the state is running new shelter camps to provide a civilized alternative to squalid grower housing, or to roosting in cars and under bridges which workers may be forced to do during peak harvest seasons.

Working with four county medical societies, the state public health department has set up twenty peak season and seven permanent medical clinics, which operate at night, rely heavily on Spanish-speaking aides, and provide free medical care, particularly for the children, among whom poor diet and neglect of dental and eye care are still chronic. In addition, federally financed compensatory education is being given to pre-school and school-aged youngsters, backed up by a brave, though not always successful attempt on the part of California, Arizona, Washington, and Delaware to keep track of their movements and continue to provide health and education programs geared to their needs.

Just as vigorously as she is tackling poverty, California is also trying to cope with crime. And with good reason: the latest (1966) figures show that her serious crime rate is now the highest in the nation, with an incidence of 2,825.7 per 100,000.

From 1961–66 several thousands of the more hopeful inmates, i.e., those expected to have success on parole, have been put through the ICE (Increased Correctional Effectiveness) program at minimum custody camps attached to major state prisons and forestry camps. The aim of ICE was to provide group living that was more helpful and more civilized than the usual incarceration—a five-day work week in pleasanter surroundings, backed up with intensive group therapy and regular community and family meetings. This, it was hoped, would begin to break down the "bad guys vs. good guys" attitude that pervades prison society, and improve behavior so that the total time served could be reduced. And it worked. A 1962–64 study showed that the total time served by all California's inmate population was cut by 1.4 months, saving the state $14 million; there was no worsening of parole by ICE graduates, and in fact these performed slightly better than ordinary inmates. Also, the program offered the researchers a positive field day.

For example, Harry A. Wilmer, a professor of psychiatry and consultant to the Department of Corrections, ran an unusual experiment in family counseling that yielded valuable information about the most neglected victims of today's crime, inmates' children. From March, 1964, to March, 1965, he organized monthly meetings at San Quentin attended by thirteen inmates, their wives, and thirty-five children aged two to seventeen. He found that about half had never been told "daddy was in prison" but had been fobbed off with some story about his being away sick or working. Living with their parents' lie made children desperately insecure, resulting in delinquency and other behavior problems, which were severely aggravated if they later discovered the truth. Facing the situation honestly brought relief all around, and as mutual problems were discussed, a lot of the bad behavior cleared up.

A similarly dismal situation was uncovered by Serapio R. Zalba during a two-year-study of 840 women felons at California Institution for Women, and their children. Family breakup was more obvious, not only because the mothers were absent, but because three-quarters had a history of marital instability and deviance, ranging from narcotics and alcoholism to prostitution or suicide attempts. Their children were bundled off to relations, mostly grandparents, and foster homes, or left at home with father. Hardly any were told the truth, though 40 per cent of them eventually guessed. As a result, about one third developed obvious emotional and health problems.

Though the ICE program ended officially in June, 1966, many of its elements are being built permanently into prison life. State prisons are being steadily decentralized under a "unitization" program, which will create a less impersonal atmosphere, and bring staff and inmates into more human contact. For example, San Quentin is being organized into five "villages" (the old cell blocks), each under a larger, permanent staff, including five counselors. Also, group therapy has been increased to include more than half (17,000) of all California inmates, and parole caseloads slashed so that half the total number of parolees belong to groups of thirty-seven instead of over seventy.

Another bold experiment was a feasibility study for a four-year college at San Quentin, conducted by the University of California extension and criminology departments, and the state department of corrections.

Years ago, bright convicts like Malcolm X, Carryl Chessman, and the Birdman of Alcatraz proved that prison can be an excellent place to get an education, except that they had no diploma to show for their pains, merely a stack of library slips. As the *Bayview Foghorn,* the San Quentin newspaper, put it, "often a bright and serious mind, out of necessity, goes out on parole as a dishwasher, or as a second-hand clothing salesman." Today, the situation has improved somewhat. About thirty prisons offer correspondence courses; nineteen offer extension courses; three or four bus men to nearby colleges, and three plug into TV study programs attached to neighboring universities.

These, however, tend to operate in obscurity. The San Quentin experiment was well publicized—and had the interest and financial support of the Ford Foundation. For five semesters inmates (and staff) were offered courses in foreign languages, literature, math, social psychology, or chemistry. By the time the study was over, a handful of students had won places at outside colleges and universities, to be claimed on release or parole. Of course, the fact that a small minority of inmates are capable of a college education and anxious to get one will not surprise too many people on the inside . . . but if a Ford Foundation-backed study confirms it, the Establishment may be convinced, with the possibility of a serious attempt to integrate the nation's prisons into the higher education system.

Crime in California is being fought with research, with therapy, with money, and above all with the willingness to experiment. It is also being fought in the field of public health, in the uneasy area where law and medicine are still struggling to rearrange the rules. The principal battleground is, of course, alcoholism.

In California, the problem is the same as elsewhere—only a little worse. Alcoholism is increasing, both because more people are taking to drink, and more problem drinkers are coming for treatment. The state has an estimated 1,275,000 people who either drink to excess, are dangerously ill, or permanently incapacitated by their drinking. This is one of the highest incidences in the nation—while San Francisco, where more than one in ten of the adult population drinks to excess, is America's booziest city. One third of the prison population has a drinking problem; half the total arrests are for drunkenness, principally drunken driving; 20 per cent of those admitted to mental hospitals are alcoholics, and the total bill to the state from driving accidents, jails, medical and welfare expenses, absenteeism, and lost productivity is nearly $1 billion a year. As usual, treatment is complicated by lack of facilities, by the reluctance of the medical profession to handle these difficult, unmotivated patients, and by sending alchoholic offenders to jail, either because this is the law or because there is nowhere else to send them.

However, a quiet revolution is taking place in federal and state handling of the problem, with California well to the fore. While most states have some sort of official program, none is quite so thorough as here. The 1965 McAteer Act, which came into operation in the summer of 1966, set up a Division of Alcoholism in the State Department of Public Health, replacing the Alcoholic Rehabilitation Division, and with wider powers to set up and maintain a comprehensive statewide program of prevention and treatment, to assist local programs, and to encourage research. The act also laid down new, tough guidelines for community programs. To qualify for funding, these must provide case-finding, including court screening procedures; diagnosis, evaluation and referral, medical treatment and counseling, including follow-up, psychiatric help, and vocational rehabilitation and employment. Money, alas, has been restricted: out of requests totaling $7 million, $1.24 million was funded in 1966, $2.5 million in 1967, and $2.64 million in 1968. Currently, nine counties are receiving funding, eight more have plans which are approved but are awaiting more state or federal money, and another fifteen are more or less actively interested in participating.

The act also created the Co-ordinating Council on Alcohol Problems, which in 1967 completed a study of changes needed in public policy. Recommendations included legislation to establish a plea of involuntary intoxication, and let alcoholics go for medical treatment instead of to jail; more state money to boost local programs, and for new and extended methods of teaching the public, especially the young, about the dangers of alcoholism. The council's report also hammered home the connection between alcoholism, illness, poverty, and crime. Together with the findings of the five-year-old Co-operative Commission on the Study of Alcoholism, centered at Stanford University, released in December, 1967, this California study will make a big contribution to current thinking on the subject.

Five years ago the case of Robinson vs. the State of California established the precedent that drug addiction is a disease, not an offense. Since then the state has continued its pioneering work, developing a public treatment system for addicts, which though far from perfect, is perhaps the most successful in the country.

The California Rehabilitation Center at Corona, east Los Angeles, and its new subsidiary center, work on the principle that addicts are sick; that treatment takes a long time, meanwhile society must be protected from them, in view of the high correlation between addiction and crime; that they must be followed up closely on release, and returned for treatment if they slip. Within the limits of confinement, addicts are provided with a campus-like setting, a pleasant community, including library, TV, movies, and provision for hobbies and further education, and group therapy to try to uncover and change the personality problems that caused "the habit." On release, generally after twelve to fourteen months, they are placed on strict parole for three years, and if they are having adjustment troubles, can stay in one of two halfway houses in Los Angeles. Everyone gets surprise nalline tests and urinalyses to find out whether they have really kicked their habit. If they haven't, they go back for further treatment. In fact, 30 per cent of them are cured, or at present capacity one a day, which is good, though it can barely keep pace with the state's 25,000 addicts.

Synanon, founded in California in 1958, claims an all over cure rate of about 50 per cent, and 90 per cent among those who stay three months or longer, thanks to its unique community living arrangements and ruthless "gut-level" therapy. Today, Synanon has houses in Santa Monica, San Diego, San Francisco, and Marshall, treating about seven hundred people. It would do more if extra funds were forthcoming—though as a system it remains of limited application since it rejects addicts who are poorly motivated or unsuited to community living. Despite all disadvantages, however, both private and public systems are spreading outside the state. Synanon has established houses in Reno and New York, while the state system has been introduced into New York.

With addiction on the way to being controlled, California is now trying to cope with the newer and often disastrous experimentation with barbiturates, amphetamines, and LSD. At the official level, an October, 1966, state law made it an offense to possess, sell, or intend to sell drugs in these categories outside fifty-seven approved hospitals, bringing California into line with the federal government, New York, and Nevada, which have similar legislation.

Unofficially, a handful of private organizations are working on the depressing but more realistic premise that some people are going to play around with drugs come what may, and need help, particularly during bad trips. In the San Francisco Bay Area, emergency help is provided by LSD Rescue, the Free Church Switch, and Drug Crisis Intervention, and (when not flopping for lack of funds) the free medical clinic in the Haight-Ashbury district. In the experience of LSD Rescue at least, experimentation with pot and LSD is definitely on the increase—among groups ranging from dentists to students at San Francisco State (30-40 per cent of whom are using pot, according to one survey) and even Hell's Angels, now stoned 90 per cent of the time and less anti-Nazi since they went on LSD.

Drugs, alcoholism and crime are all well known family splitters, along with money troubles, mobility, insecurity, immaturity, and other intangibles. In an effort to heal California's broken marriages—the divorce rate is 2.9 per 1,000 population, compared with the national average of 2.3 per 1,000—former Governor Brown created a special commission on the family, which reported in December, 1966.

The eighteen-man commission made three important recommendations. First, the need for a family court, with jurisdiction over all family matters ranging from marriage to the division of property and the guardianship of minors. In addition, the court would offer counseling by a specially-trained staff aimed at preventing family breakdown. Second, the law should be changed to eliminate the legal idea of "fault" as the basis for divorce. Dissenting couples would have to prove to the family court that their marriage had broken down, rather than citing adultery, cruelty, or desertion. Third, the need for uniform custody laws throughout the United States—a proposal which was laid before the Commission on Uniform State Laws.

Implementation of these humane recommendations is, at present, extremely uncertain. A bill along these lines in 1967 was sent by the state legislature for interim study, a polite form of limbo. A second bill is due to be introduced in 1968, but, in the view of Richard Dinkelspiel, co-chairman of the original commission, its chances are not good, thanks to gubernatorial apathy, and the general reluctance on the part of legislators and public to alter their thinking on so vital and intimate a subject. The only consolation is that the whole report has been submitted to the Commision on Uniform State Laws, which is currently working on a national study of our divorce laws.

Meanwhile, the State Department of Health's Bureau of Vital Statistics is compiling an unprecedentedly thorough series of socio-economic figures on divorce, separation, and annulment. Though California is the twenty-sixth state to join the Federal Divorce Register, it is the only one to ask couples wishing to separate to state their occupation, length of residence, previous marriages, race, color ("my color is peach"), religion, educational level, number and ages of children, and when the couple married and separated. When the computers have done their stuff, the result may be a unique set of analytic and predictive tables, throwing new light on family breakdown.

While society is becoming more aware of the problems of the two-generation family, it is also giving top priority to the generation left behind, euphemistically called our "senior citizens." As Medicare and the new community mental health centers become well established, fresh problems are arising. How can a high quality of medical care be maintained without overloading existing facilities? Public hospitals are already overcrowded; is there any way to screen off the less seriously ill and treat them privately or at home? While acute physical illness is easier to detect, mental illness is more elusive, especially in older people suffering the side effects of congestive heart failure, diabetes, alcoholism, and malnutrition.

A research project at the San Francisco Langley Porter Hospital, headed by Mrs. Marjorie Lowenthal and Dr. Alexander Smith, has done a lot to solve this difficulty. It consisted of a survey of 1,200 over-65's, half supposedly healthy and half in the hospital psychiatric wards, done at three points in time, beginning in 1959. Researchers found that 86 per cent of the hospitalized sample were in need of full time care, more than half being in a state of crisis, 28 per cent having a chronic brain disorder and 19 per cent a psychogenic disorder without brain damage. Fifteen per cent of the community sample were psychiatrically impaired, but only one was in need of full time hospital treatment.

The survey confirmed suspicions that many elderly people need full time care, though not necessarily in a hospital. To decide who should go where, Mrs. Lowenthal and her team devised a simple but accurate series of tests to screen off the most seriously mentally ill, based on thirteen questions that can elicit the difference between brain and non-brain damage. As a result of this discovery, the hospital created a geriatric screening unit, and admissions have dropped drastically. During the fall of 1966 it went a step further and started one of the country's first geriatric outpatient clinics.

Mrs. Lowenthal's surveys also exposed as fallacies some well established thinking about older people and their problems. In the first place, there is little evidence of the "dumping" of older folk by exasperated or exhausted families. "It is astonishing what families went through to avoid sending someone to the psychiatric ward," commented Mrs. Lowenthal. "The person who made the recommendation was usually the physician. The family tried all sorts of possibilities but they didn't work."

Retirement is not necessarily the emotional shock it is believed to be, according to a related study of the morale of the community sample. Oddly enough, it seems to be more damaging to the working women than the men, possibly because they are subject to a conflict in life styles which comes home to roost in old age. Detailed results are appearing in four separate volumes, and will include a plea for more research, better treatment facilities, and a less ambiguous attitude to elderly people by the medical profession, which has a noticeable lack of enthusiasm for geriatrics.

The main stumbling block to California's immediate future as a pacemaker to social change is Governor Reagan, his faceless advisors, and the increased Republican representation at the legislature.

Since taking over in January, 1967, the governor has been obsessed with the idea of economy, not in itself a bad notion, but here directed mainly at higher education and social services. The result has been a discouraging frost, stunting the full growth of the new careers and alcoholism programs, closing seven out of the thirteen multi-service centers, freezing the findings of the commission on the family, and slashing the Consumer Counsel budget to an idiotically low level.

Certain Reagan appointments have proved injudicious, not to say disastrous. At San Quentin, the tough new warden Louis "Big Red" Nelson has been unsympathetic to reform and his regime provoked the strike in February, 1968, in support of better conditions. Mrs. Kay Valory, the new Consumer Counsel (formerly co-chairman of the Reagan Inaugural Committee) has antagonized consumers by appearing to spend more time attending businessmen's meetings than working for their welfare. Reagan himself has done a first-rate job of offending people, either by personal rudeness (when he accused former governor Brown of "looting" the state budget), by his handling of student unrest at the University of California and his personal vote for the dismissal of Clark Kerr, and the series of economies suggested by "Reagan's Raiders," executives on loan from prominent California corporations, whose presence caused even quite moderate liberals to speculate whether the businessmen weren't taking over the state entirely.

Research into social problems will, of course, go on, since it is as much a state product as aerospace or oranges. To what extent the man at the top can really rock the boat will be decided during the remaining years of Reagan's office. Meanwhile the liberals are moaning but making the best of it, even though, like Alice, they are having to run twice as hard to stay in the same place.

James P. Degnan

SANTA CRUZ:
A WORKABLE UTOPIA

To grow large while seeming small, to combine the virtues of the big university with those of the small liberal arts college, and above all, to give high quality undergraduate education in the liberal arts are the goals of the University of California at Santa Cruz—the most unusual state university in the nation.

In large part, the University at Santa Cruz is a reaction to the specialization and vocationalism that for many years have made a farce of the liberal arts and, in so doing, a farce of undergraduate education in our state colleges and universities. As critics like Hutchins, Barzun, Whyte, Bestor, Rickover, and others have amply demonstrated, instead of being required to spend four years of rigorous work in basic liberal arts disciplines, e.g., language, science, history, math, literature, and philosophy, the typical American undergraduate—the individual who attends

State U. to prepare for a job as an engineer, dentist, businessman, football coach or whatever—gets away with taking a few required liberal arts courses (courses which, because they are required, are usually watered down), and then proceeds to spend the remainder of his college career taking courses in his major, i.e., vocational rather than liberal arts courses, the former often being utter nonsense, as are many, if not most, courses in business and education: Methods in Minor Sports, Principles of Advertising, Resort Club Accounting, Purchasing School Supplies, etc. That such an undergraduate regularly emerges from four years of college a sub-literate or a technical barbarian, e.g., an engineer with little moral and less aesthetic intelligence (Highway Departments, California's being a prime example, are full of these) is not surprising. At Santa Cruz the vocationalism that helps to produce such mental and moral defectives has been eliminated. At Santa Cruz there are no undergraduate vocational majors, e.g., no business, engineering, education and physical education majors. The student entering Santa Cruz can look forward to four years of intense, serious (though often unconventional) interdisciplinary work in the liberal arts.

More important, however, than what subjects are taught at Santa Cruz is how those subjects are taught. Convinced that genuine high quality liberal arts education is difficult if not impossible (even in first-rate private universities) in the usual American university atmosphere of crowded lecture halls, of endless pressures to take notes, pass tests, and write papers all in order to get grades, of moronic wastes of time generated by competitive college athletics, Santa Cruz, designed like Oxford as a series of small independent non-departmental colleges, each with its own provost and faculty, emphasizes the small seminar and independent study. More impersonal forms of instruction such as the lecture are used but only to conserve valuable time for close teaching. Moreover, at Santa Cruz, although the students are required to take thirty-six courses during their four years (courses often interdisciplinary in nature) and to have a major, conventional letter grades are not usually assigned. Students are simply given "Pass" or "Fail" grades, and much of the pressure of studying simply for grades is thus removed. Instead of a letter grade, each student will have in his file a written evaluation from each of his instructors, a letter which should provide a more accurate guide to the student's ability than does the conventional grade. Instead of the onerous round of quizzes, tests, etc., Santa Cruz stresses such methods of evaluating the student's performance as the seminar report, the short critical or research paper, and, perhaps most important, the comprehensive exam which every student must pass before receiving his degree. Finally, with the exception of intramurals—for which excellent facilities are provided—Santa Cruz has eliminated the playground atmosphere and academic abuses which usually derive from "big-time" athletics programs, by not permitting such programs. At Santa Cruz there are no coaching staffs, no major athletic events with other colleges, and no facilities, such as stadiums, for large numbers of spectators.

Located on the site of the old Cowell Ranch and lime quarry— 2,000 acres of timber and meadowland in the mountainous coastal area between Carmel and San Francisco—the campus at Santa Cruz overlooks the Pacific and is as beautiful as its educational plan is unique. Above all the Santa Cruz campus is a lesson in intelligent land conservation and use, a lesson California—a state which has destroyed more natural beauty and more natural resources more rapidly than any comparable territory in history— badly needs. Since the end of World War II when land speculators and developers began "The Destruction of California," to quote Raymond Dasmann's title, since California began, "Going, Going," the state's best planners—men like Karl Belser of Santa Clara County—have argued that with intelligent planning, e.g., zoning laws, tax reforms, etc., California could accommodate its increasing population as well as its new industry and still preserve most of its irreplaceable natural resources and incomparable natural beauty, that California could have, in short, the best of the present and the past. But voices like Mr. Belser's—voices with no real political or economic weight behind them—were lost in the babbling wilderness of land speculators, of real estate, concrete, asphalt and bulldozer interests. Southern California was destroyed, and a good part of Northern California, the San Francisco Bay Area, including Mr. Belser's own Santa Clara Valley, has been transformed needlessly and mindlessly into a hideous, smog-covered, amoeboid sprawl of housing tracts, freeways and shopping centers. A land development like the campus at Santa Cruz is a monument of refutation to those who say that population increases automatically mean the destruction of natural beauty, and a monument of justification to the wisdom as well as to the long and seemingly futile struggle of planners like Mr. Belser.

Expected to grow from its present 1,900 students and three colleges (Cowell, Adlai E. Stevenson, and Crown) to 27,500 students and twenty or more colleges in the next thirty years, Santa Cruz is skillfully planned not only to preserve the natural beauty and character of its site, but to enhance that beauty and character. The campus at Santa Cruz, unlike the usual California land development, conforms to and co-operates with, rather than dominates and destroys, its natural setting. Its magnificent trees, redwood and madrone and live oak and fir, many of them 150 years or more in age, and its fields of wildflowers with their Oz-like coloring are rigorously protected from the axe and bulldozer; its roads are narrow and winding, designed more for the pedestrian or bicyclist than for the automobile; (Santa Cruz students are discouraged from driving or having automobiles on campus); its sheer ravines and gulleys instead of being filled have, when necessary, been tastefully bridged, and one of its two old quarries has been ingeniously converted into a natural outdoor theater; its weathered fences and wooden and stone ranch buildings instead of being razed have been rehabilitated, the old buildings being used for offices and for storage space. And its new buildings—those of the three colleges now operating, plus two science halls, the University Library, and other buildings in progress including those of a fourth college to open in 1968— seem as indigenous to their surroundings as do the old structures. New and experimental, they possess that architectural magic which makes them appear to belong where they are and—rarity of rarities for California—to have been there for a while. The first commandment for architects at Santa Cruz has been that since any attempt to "compete with the natural grandeur of this site is doomed to failure" architectural efforts shall be concentrated on creating buildings that relate to the site and that give outward expression to and make physically possible the educational philosophy of the university. So far, the commandment has been obeyed.

Architecturally, the educational goals of "combining the virtues of the big university with those of the small liberal arts college" and of "growing large yet seeming small" are achieved in this way: The colleges surround, in a scattered but unified arrangement, a core of buildings common to big universities: a central library, labs, administrative buildings and the buildings of professional schools which will open in coming years; yet each college is self-contained. Besides having a distinct architecture and a distinct curriculum, each college has its own residence facilities, its own dining hall, and, of course, its own liberal arts faculty, e.g., its own faculty of math, language, science, philosophy, and literature teachers. Theoretically—although the student will probably want to cross college lines to take various courses and will be encouraged to do so—the student could spend his four years in the college he enters; and this, plus the fact that no college will ever exceed an enrollment of 1,000, even when the university attains its maximum enrollment in 1995 or thereabouts, guarantees that the student will always enjoy the sense of belonging to a university which "seems small" even as it "grows large." Further, the colleges are designed architecturally to create an atmosphere which bridges the gap between "learning and leisure," an atmosphere totally conducive to the liberal arts education, an atmosphere which relates faculty and students, not only inside the classroom but outside as well. The colleges are designed to encourage the "easy and natural" kind of informal learning that takes place over coffee or in the dining hall. Some faculty will actually live in the college residence halls; some—including all provosts of the various colleges—will have homes on campus and will be reasonably available to the students of their respective colleges.

Despite its idyllic setting and its unique and exciting educational plan, the University at Santa Cruz has, and will undoubtedly continue to have, major problems. For one, although San Francisco is not far away—75 miles or so—and although the University at Santa Cruz may well be the beginning of a new and exciting cultural area in California (about which, more later), students and faculty desiring easy access to a real cosmopolitan area aren't going to find it at Santa Cruz, not for sometime to come, anyway. The physical remoteness of the university plus the natural provincialism of the California student aggravated by his feeling that at Santa Cruz he belongs to an elite of educational pioneers, some Santa Cruz faculty feel, may breed in the Santa Cruz student a provincial smugness; however, to combat this, there are already tentative plans for an "extra-mural" program that will get the Santa Cruz students "out from under the redwoods" into jobs in the larger society or periods of study at other universities. Further, some faculty feel that the informal atmosphere of close contact between undergraduates and professors Santa Cruz encourages, easily degenerates into chumminess and anti-intellectualism and that this is already a problem at Santa Cruz. These faculty members, like many other critics, contend—with justification—that far too many contemporary undergraduates—especially California's who are products of probably the most permissive society in the nation—already have far too high an opinion of themselves, an opinion too often inflated by the high grades they've been given for mediocre efforts by mediocre teachers in mediocre high schools. To these young people, intellectual humility (or any other kind) is a sickness; they are raised to believe that their "opinion is as good as anyone's." Bright they may be, but intellectually (as well as sartorially) they tend to be an unbuttoned, sloppy breed who come to the university with not the slightest conception of work or of intellectual discipline. This, in part, explains why they so often feel free to denigrate anything and anybody including their elders, their instructors, and their unquestionable superiors—the world's greatest thinkers and artists. To encourage rather than to eradicate these vices, some faculty believe, may be an unintended and harmful effect of the Santa Cruz atmosphere. Furthermore, too much emphasis by the administration on "informal, personal relationships" between teachers and students, some believe, can scare off desirable faculty. A top scholar-teacher pondering whether or not to come to Santa Cruz may actually like the Santa Cruz rule that its faculty must be both first-rate teachers and scholars, that, in short, at Santa Cruz teaching-research is a 50-50 matter. (This is in contrast to many universities where scholars can get by with a 10 per cent teaching load, plus mediocre teaching, providing the other 90 per cent of their time is spent producing scholarship that will give the university "national visibility.") And such a teacher-scholar may actually like the idea of the college—an interdisciplinary group of faculty, rather than a department—judging his teaching and of a combination university–college board of peers in his field judging his scholarship, but he may well resent the idea that if he is to be judged a top teacher he must spend substantial time outside the classroom fraternizing with the students.

At Santa Cruz, however, these problems rather than getting worse, will probably be attenuated. If, for instance, one of the early colleges makes the mistake of creating too "chummy" an atmosphere it can, of course, always reform; but even if it doesn't, students and faculty disdainful of "chumminess" may have the opportunity of selecting another college at Santa Cruz. Thus bigness at Santa Cruz—instead of being the vice it is at most state universities—may well prove a virtue.

All in all, the real wisdom of Santa Cruz, its real uniqueness, is that unlike other rather Utopian experiments in American liberal arts education—e.g., Hutchins' Chicago experiment, various Great Books experiments, Santa Cruz is flexible, non-doctrinaire, and free to create rather than forced to reform. Among the many problems facing Hutchins at Chicago was that he could not start fresh; he had to reform the institution, to "persuade," for example, the faculty already there that what he wanted to do was desirable. Further, a weakness of Hutchins' and other similar experiments is that they are almost always inflexible and doctrinaire, Procrustean Beds based on dogma like *"The* truth is that of Aristotle perfected by Aquinas . . . " or *"The* Great Books are . . . ," etc. That such experiments bog down in futile argument and bickering is not surprising. Unlike Hutchins at Chicago, Dean McHenry, Chancellor at the University at Santa Cruz, started Santa Cruz literally from the ground up and he started it with men—many of them from Harvard and Yale—who were in general agreement with him about the nature and major goals of the University. But while there has been a general agreement as to the ends of the University at Santa Cruz, there has, by no means, been agreement as to the ways of achieving these ends. Thus, for a university that offers a most traditional kind of education, there is, at Santa Cruz, a healthy respect for and even encouragement of innovation and unconventional approaches to that education. As Byron Stookey, Santa Cruz's young Director of Academic Planning says: "Santa Cruz is an unconventional venture" which requires men of "unconventional vision." A look at the colleges the university plans to begin in the next ten years—all colleges devoted to the goal of offering high quality liberal arts education for undergraduates—reveals the truth of Mr. Stookey's remark. There is talk of colleges that would give special attention to international affairs, to our natural environment and resources, or to urban problems. In these colleges the traditional approach to the liberal arts—an approach which because it proceeds from past to present, from universal to particular, lacks relevance for many contemporary students—may be reversed, i.e., students in the college of urban affairs may begin their studies with the specific contemporary problem of rehabilitating a neighborhood or town or city, and in the course of solving the problem will begin naturally to raise and to attempt to answer the questions upon which the liberal arts education is based: What is man? What is the good society? What is the relationship of man to God? What is the Good? Who should own the world's wealth?, etc. That it requires a top faculty—an extremely responsible as well as imaginative and talented faculty—and a top student body to make such an approach work is undeniable. But it is just such a faculty and student body that Santa Cruz is designed to attract.

Finally, the great charm of the University at Santa Cruz like the charm of the area in which it is located, is that it is still, in scholastic terms, "pure potency"; it can become whatever it wants to become. The university can certainly become a great liberal arts institution, an institution which may begin a revitalization of the moribund liberal arts programs all over the nation and an institution which may begin major reforms in the highly specialized programs of American graduate schools. And it can become a great and unique conservation and planning center, a center where planners can be liberally educated rather than—as is too often the case today—technically trained. Further, the university could well become the beginning of an exciting civilization. I refer to the Monterey Bay–Santa Cruz area. One of the world's most beautiful locales, it is jeopardized by the builders and land speculators who have destroyed much of California north of the University at Santa Cruz; however, because there is much wealth in the Monterey-Carmel area, preserving that area, i.e., getting zoning laws, conservation easements, etc., should not be nearly so difficult as preserving most areas of California. The university might well lead the battle to preserve and then to culturally develop the Santa Cruz–Monterey Bay area.

Archibald MacLeish has said that the University of California was built to face the future. America will watch the University of California at Santa Cruz with the hope that it will not only face but help to shape the future.

John Bright

DISNEY'S

FANTASY EMPIRE

Walt Disney, grand vizier of fantasy, possessed the world's largest collection of personal honoraria—praise emblazoned on plaques, medals, cups, scrolls, statuettes and testimonials. Shortly before he died, Uncle Walt, as he was known to his professional family, assigned a woman to organize and ,annotate the laurels. She worked a year at it, full time.

Most of these evidences of approval came from such sources as the Motion Picture Academy (which handed more Oscars to Disney than to any score of film people), distributors, chambers of commerce, fraternal lodges, cities, states, even nations. Some of these may be suspect as motivated by flackery, or impersonal

---

This article was conceived as a critique of a man, his works and organization. The recent death of Walt Disney necessitated not only changes in tense but a look at the Fantasy Empire's future. No other revisions of fact, opinion or judgment are imperative.—*The Author.*

business gratitude. (Disney's public relations machinery was the best in the field. Henceforward it may be a little like Christianity without Christ.) Not so the thumping superlative of Dr. Max Rafferty, boss of California's sophomores, who once said that "Disney is the greatest educator of the century."

If this compliment seems tarnished by the dubious authority of its tosser, a similar garland was pitched by David Low, the respected British cartoonist, who elevated Disney to be "the most significant figure in graphic art since Leonardo." No art critics squirmed in protest, perhaps because they read their own meaning into Low's "significant."

Educators, however, took Rafferty's goose grease at its full value. Librarian Frances Clarke Sayers of UCLA blasted the "absurd appraisal." "In the Disney films," she wrote, "I find genuine feeling ignored, the imagination of children bludgeoned with mediocrity, and much of it overcast with vulgarity. Look at the wretched sprite with the wand and the oversized buttocks which announces every Disney program on TV. She is a vulgar little thing who has been too long at the sugar bowls."

Dr. Benjamin Spock deplored the sadism in many of the Disney cartoons, citing the Wicked Witch in *Snow White* as a terrifying figure for young children, reporting that "Nelson Rockefeller told my wife a long time ago that they had to reupholster the seats in Radio City Music Hall after *Snow White* because they were wet so often by frightened children." (The present writer witnessed an almost fatal attack of juvenile hysteria in a Mexico City theater when Pinocchio was swallowed by the whale.)

Disneyland, too, has produced a chorus of outrage. John Ciardi, driven into verbal murk by his distaste, noted in the *Saturday Review* that he was "ready to see him [Disney] as the incarnate myth of all that is naturally depthless," then added sourly: "I saw instead the shyster in the backroom of the illusion, diluting his witch's brew with tap water, while all his gnomes worked frantically to design a gaudier and gaudier design for the mess."

Julian Halevy (in *The Nation,* June 7, 1958) suffered a socio-philosophical recoil from the fantasy Mecca, where "the whole world, the universe, and all man's dominion over self and nature has been reduced to a sickening blend of cheap formulas packaged to sell." Equating Disneyland with Las Vegas he intoned ominously: "Their huge profits and mushrooming growth suggest that as conformity and adjustment become more rigidly imposed on the American scene the drift to fantasy will become a flight."

The article drew fire from Ray Bradbury who wrote an *ad hominem* letter to *The Nation,* concluding with his "sneaking suspicion . . . that Mr. Halevy loved Disneyland but is not man enough, or child enough, to admit it." Later Bradbury aired his own feelings about the park for *Holiday,* in rhapsodic prose more imaginative than anything of Uncle Walt's.

I tend to side with Bradbury and the new masses on this issue. Halevy's analogy is snobbery and spurious. Las Vegas is Western civilization at its cynical worst, a reduction of man's dignity to an alienating scramble for a dirty, desperate buck. It is truly narcotic, neurotic, unreal but not fantasy. Disneyland, to adults, who almost outnumber the delighted kids, is a retreat (or escape, if you will) from the anxieties of that scramble and the conformities it imposes. All escape is not neurotic. What's sick about a vacation?

There is here a germane paradox: while the films and the park were both Disney's deeply personal creations—and while in some ways they overlap as reflections of his attitudes—most of the criticisms that can reasonably be leveled at the movies simply do not apply to Disneyland.

Item: It is the only major amusement park in America which does not stimulate and capitalize upon hostile aggression and competitiveness. Nor upon fright. Its thrills (except to over-grownups like Ciardi and Halevy) are derived from and targeted to the child in us. I'm sure Dr. Spock would concur.

Item: Disneyland is relatively free of appeals to chauvinism and racism. The qualification is necessitated by an "Aunt Jemima" restaurant, a suspicious paucity of Negro help, even in the unskilled functions, and several concessions to stereotype: e.g., panicky blacks from a safari pursued by wild animals and climbing a totem pole having a white man symbolically at the top; and an exhibit of birds from different countries that speak English in stereotypical accents—*mañana* Mexicans, oo-la-la Frenchmen, pidgin Chinese, etc. The patronizing is not blatant, but it has a cumulative effect. Nevertheless, "It's a Small World" is more representative of the park's overall tone. Here the singing and dancing doll-children of the earth—white and black, brown and yellow—are equally attractive and charming. It is the one-world concept applied to a child's dream of a toy store come wondrously to life. The "adventure," originally presented in New York at the fair, scarcely reflected Uncle Walt's political views, so there may have been a liberal Moses in the bulrushes. (The commercial sponsor of the exhibit is the Bank of America, thinking globally these days since going international, with branches and agents everywhere this side of the dollar curtain.)

Item: Through the most intelligently managed system of controls—from parking to adventuring and dining—an entirely new kind of crowd behavior is stimulated. The same people who grow raucously assertive at ball games and prize fights, and in other amusement parks, here comport themselves with a conspicuous good nature and freedom from irritation that has been remarked by observers less than by biased press agents. Squalling infants, even at fatigue peak in the evening hours, are rare. The park's ban on alcohol, determined by its family orientation, reduces hooliganism to a minimum. In 1965 there was only one "rumble" in Disneyland, and it was swiftly suppressed, without counter violence. Last year was altogether untroubled. The almost Dutch cleanliness of the pavement and exhibits, under ceaseless janitoring, is contagious. People respond, consciously or otherwise, to their surroundings. Do you see cigarette butts and beer cans in a cemetery? Perhaps Khrushchev's eagerness to visit the park betrayed more than the roly-poly child in Nikita, and was to verify spy rumors that this was capitalist crowd handling at its smoothest—a technique applicable to his own centers of culture and rest. In a nation of endless queues, so corrupting to tempers and morale, Disneyland has devised a pattern of narrow-railed aisles, humorously suggesting a rat maze, and creating the illusion of a short line.

Item: There is a fixed policy of no-pitch, no-hustle. Instead of the pock-nosed carnies of boardwalk familiarity, fresh-faced youngsters, recruited mainly from the neighboring colleges, are given a six-week course in manners at the "University of Disneyland," and emerge as courteous as librarians.

Item: No gangsters, frontier or modern, are glorified. The park's only historical hero is Abe Lincoln, an astonishingly (even disturbingly) lifelike robot animated in speech and movement with electronic sorcery. The sponsor of the Great Emancipator spectacle, not surprisingly, is Lincoln Savings.

Offsetting these virtues, many critics remark the middle-class, somewhat shallow and anti-intellectual, character of the Disney entertainment product. One of the qualities of its babbittry is a stubborn, uncritical optimism: things are getting better and better; what's faulty will inevitably be corrected. An amusing illustration of this is in "Rocket to the Moon," a simulated space ride in that section of the Disney pie called Tomorrowland. It is circa 1970, and the taped voice of the alleged captain of the vessel proclaims as we approach home: "That cloudy mass you see on the earth is not smog—it is a bank of clouds. Smog was eliminated in North America some time ago." The audience (passengers) laughed. To their inflamed eyes this was wishful thinking. To Disney it was prophecy.

Disney's films have come in for a similar but heavier bombardment from the educated. Again to quote Dr. Sayers, whose misgivings are typical:

> I think Disney falsifies life by pretending that everything is so sweet, so saccharine, without any conflict except the obvious conflict of violence. I think that even in the lines of Mother Goose you find an element that is in all great literature, and that is the

realization that in life is a tragic tension between good and evil, between disaster and triumph, and it isn't all a matter of sweetness and light. The first people to know this intuitively are the children themselves. . . . This, I think, is the tragic break in Disney. He misplaces the sweetness and misplaces the violence, and the result is like soap opera, not really related to the great truths of life.

The Sayers anger might be extended to the bedrock Hollywood rationalization: "We have to give them what they want if we are to stay in business!" It overlooks the point that having retarded the child, our alternative is to cater to his deficiency. He wants what he has been taught to want.

To all such diatribes Disney responded with mild hurt and dismay; and a kind of bewilderment, since his belief in movies and television as solely entertainment was sincere. And because he was the only producer whose name on the marquee sold tickets (except possibly De Mille, another treacle salesman), his policy was fortified by the primary American judgment: what makes money must be good. Al Capone once put it to this writer: "How can a million dollars be wrong?"

Until his last illness Uncle Walt was reputed to be a happy uncle. He may have had dark moments in his private projection room, but he was smilingly insistent that happiness pervade his films, like a permanent Edgar Guest in the house. Motion pictures accounted for 46 per cent of his happily diversified empire; TV contributed 8 per cent more. Some indication of the cash value of happiness is the box-office intake of *Mary Poppins,* a gross approaching $50 million, with more ahead from reissue and eventual television rights. *That Darn Cat* is expected to do almost as well.

Until two decades ago, Disney catered very little to the national sweet tooth. He concentrated, rather, upon breaking ground and ground rules. Some of his innovations were recklessly *avant-garde,* earning him pages in the journals of serious students of the cinema. Robert Feild, a Harvard professor of art, wrote a carefully researched encomium, *The Art of Walt Disney,* in 1942.

Ironically, the decline of the Disney fortunes was touched off by his first big hit, *Snow White,* which the industry looked forward to, with secret glee, as a foolish departure from convention. When the picture became a noisy success, here and abroad, Walt and his normally cautious brother, Roy, went on an inflationary spree of feature-length animated cartoons, all enormously costly. The company had gone deep into debt to build the Burbank studio, and was in a precarious position unless each of these pictures would do better than pay its way. When *Fantasia* flopped, the Disneys were in Zeckendorf-type trouble, overexpanded and with dismal credit. The bankers had, somewhat reluctantly, loaned construction money to Disney when their community studies indicated that the site he had chosen for a studio could perhaps be better used for a hospital: that explains the oversize elevators and the reception desks at both ends of all halls. There is small likelihood today of the studio's being converted into a hospital, even with Disney gone, but the bankers' researches were right: the Catholic Church has since built a hospital across the street.

In desperation the Disneys were compelled to "go public," sharing ownership and control with an army of alien stockholders. For Walt this could have meant the sacrifice of artistic freedom to avoid bankruptcy. Shareholders disapprove of experimentation with *their* money. More immediately, the situation called for severe reduction of studio overhead. Disney's behavior in this period scarcely sustains the benevolent paternalism of his sedulously nurtured image. It is missing from the swollen library of Disneyana, like George Washington's false teeth. Even John McDonald, in an otherwise excellent *Fortune* piece, ignores the salient facts and substitutes sentimentality.

Disney first confronted the crisis of 1941 in a plea to his employees—a compound of passion and anguish and charm—that they take a wage cut or face wholesale firings. Everyone chose the cut to save the job. Within a fortnight Disney violated the gentlemen's agreement by dismissing thirteen men, of whom twelve were militants in the Screen Cartoonists Guild, then seeking recognition under the Wagner Act as the bargaining agent for the animated cartoon industry. In the prolonged strike that followed, to make Disney's studio a closed shop, the rehiring of the thirteen men was a major union demand.

In *Fortune*'s account it was a "jurisdictional strike," and it added that "the event so dismayed Walt Disney that he wept." There are of course jurisdictional strikes, conflicts of power between labor blocks, but the phrase is also often used to arouse public prejudice against a legitimate walkout. As for the Disney tears, they were more likely symptoms of rage than of dismay. Filmed views of his confrontation of the picket line show him in apoplectic fury.

One of Disney's defensive measures was to exploit illusion, his specialty, as a strikebreaking weapon. The studio was 50 per cent struck. To convey the impression that only a few mavericks had gone out, photographs were taken from the air by the Los Angeles *Times,* a stern Uncle Walt having ordered that all the automobiles of the on-the-job workers and the studio cars and trucks be taken from sheds and garages and posed for the skyborne cameras.

The current obese solvency of the Disney complex (total income in 1965 was $110 million) is due only in part to the marshmallow cream puffs of intellectual disdain. The ship of fantasy is now a flotilla, all vessels controlled from a single port but each with a separate identity and cargo.

Until Disney, horizontal diversification was unknown in show business, unless popcorn can be so construed. Production and exhibition—recently divorced by a Supreme Court that has not prevented clandestine remarriage—is not diversification; it is neutral control. Roy Disney has made a brilliant application of insurance-company structuring to the entertainment field. In fact it has a tighter logic—that of fingers on a hand. Disneyland advertises Disney movies and animal personalities, Disney TV plugs the park, where commercial exhibits by TV advertisers reduce overhead and raise profits. And the same golden symbiosis applies to publications, comic strips, toys and 2,000 other products.

And yet—may not the empire crack and crumble with the death of Caesar? Stockholders and top staffers have long been worried about that, and even the atheists among them prayed for his immortality. Roy Disney may have joined them in supplication, but this did not preclude an insurance policy, with the company as beneficiary, larger than Mrs. Graham's coverage of Billy.

In my view, the apprehension is groundless. Disney Enterprises has long and widely been considered a one-man overlordship, a multiple genius surrounded by echoes. This is a dogma to make a legendary figure out of Uncle Walt. (Part of the ritual was an arrangement whereby Disney picked up all the studio Oscars, a usurpation resented by the creators.) The need for this aggrandizement stemmed in part from the studio's casting policy. Hollywood pundits say that "Disney gets them on the way up or on the way down," spurning the star system with its bloated salaries. To compete in the glamour game, Disney himself became the box-office attraction—as producer of a predictable family style and the father of a family of lovable animals.

Behind the façade has always been a legion of diverse, anonymous talents. Except for the loss of its generalissimo, this army is today intact, and with a general staff. Of the established components of the mother-lode, Disneyland now needs Disney no more than *The Saturday Evening Post* needs Ben Franklin. As for the live-action films and TV, they are also on their own, requiring to maintain altitude only an inventive mediocrity—the basic coin of Hollywood.

What may be affected (if the myth of Walt's indispensability has penetrated the banking heart) are the two gigantic projects of potential *super* profits, long on the expansionary drawing board— Mineral King and the invasion of Florida.

Closer to fruition, with ample pledged financing, Mineral King is planned as an Alpine village in the Sequoia National Forest, a year-round ski resort to accommodate 20,000 on the slopes at one time—and house and feed them. Tentative budget: $38 million. There are no insurmountable engineering difficulties; the only snag is political. An extended highway through mountain terrain is vital, and its cost would place too great an amortization burden on the resort. So the Disneys have been insisting that the state pay the bill, with an argument not altogether selfish: tourism is big business in California. Now Uncle Walt's extraordinary gifts of persuasion are missing—but so is Pat Brown. Governor Reagan will probably be happy to dedicate the road as a macadam memorial to his old friend.

More uncertain is the destiny of the Florida promotion, a jumbo Disneyland and "model city of the future," to be located near Orlando. Disney's biggest dream, the construction estimate is $500 million, it promises to ignite the biggest boom since William Jennings Bryan sold real estate in Florida.

It promises another reward for the Disneys—an atonement for the sickening mistake they made when they founded Disneyland. Building the park on cheap desert land (rather than in Burbank, the original idea) was sharp operation. But creating a powerful crowd magnet for outsiders to profit from was a galling oversight. In the last decade, a prosperous growth of hotels, motels, restaurants, gas stations and stores, even a wax museum (fantasy cribbing), have mushroomed around Disneyland. The neighboring town of Anaheim, formerly a sleepy village, is today a bustling big town, with a thriving John Birch Society chapter. It is a kind of cheating, like watching drive-in movies from outside the fence.

No such error is to tarnish the Florida triumph. Land has been bought, or optioned, in large concentric circles, including a buffer region. *This* time no pip-squeak parasites were to get rich off Uncle Walt. Now it is not certain that this sweet revenge will come to pass, but there is a straw in the wind: when news of Walt's demise came over the news ticker, the Disney stock dipped a melancholy dollar. However, it quickly rallied on the rumor of a merger with Litton Industries, a saber-toothed holding company. Such a union could signal the conquest of Florida.

Just how does one assay the Disney phenomenon? To call him a genius, as his sycophants do, is not only absurd; it is unenlightening. I think the man's unique success can be understood only by reference to his personal *non*-uniqueness. Of all the activists of public diversion, Uncle Walt was the one most precisely in the American midstream—in taste and morality, attitudes and opinions, prides and prejudices. The revealing clue is his familiar (and utterly sincere) statement that he never made a picture he didn't want his family to see. His competitors made pictures they thought, or guessed, the public wanted to see. Disney operated through maximal *identification* with John Doe; the others seek to discover what John Doe is like in order to cater to him.

The celebrated Disney inventiveness is the x-factor in the success story. A key to this might be found in his immaturity, or not realized maturity—not used here in the pejorative sense. Walt, growing from infant to child to youngster, to adult, to uncle and granduncle, never abandoned the delights and preoccupations of each stage of development, as most of us have done, at least in part. This was his "genius." Disneyland could have been created only by a man-child who never tired of toys or shed the belief that animals and insects have human attributes.

Not long ago he described his role with a characteristic metaphor:

"You know, I was stumped one day when a little boy asked, 'Do you draw Mickey Mouse?' I had to admit I didn't draw any more. 'Then you think up all the jokes and ideas?' 'No,' I said, 'I don't do that.' Finally he looked at me and said: 'Mr. Disney, just what do you do?' . . . 'Well,' I said, 'sometimes I think of myself as a little bee. I go from one area of the studio to another and gather pollen and sort of stimulate everybody. I guess that's the job I do.' "

It isn't every man who is privileged to write his own epitaph.

Richard G. Lillard

THE SOIL BENEATH
THE BLACKTOP

Ever since that fateful publicity event, the Gold Rush, California
ranching and agriculture have been special marvels. Whether expanding to grandiose proportions or contracting because of unusual disasters, they have been a conditioning part of the exceptional, imagination-catching role of California. The good earth of
the spacious Golden State, graced by the only areas of Mediter-
ranean climate in the United States, has enabled California to be
the leader of innovations in crops and marketing, in labor relations,
and in automation. The state is also a leader in obliterating the
best soils and in devising projects to rescue them and keep them
in production.

Commercial growing in California has been tied to the unparalleled variety of local climates and soils in the plains and
valleys and mountains, from the fog-cooled coasts to the hot,

wind-swept interior deserts. It is related to the limited and irregular natural water supply and the long, dry summers, which have led men to carry out extraordinary water works, pumping dry the earth's crust and creating the longest rivers in the known geological history of the state.

A century ago the problem for California agriculture was the distance between its orchards and fields and the consuming population back east. The solution was trans-continental railroads and, later, trucks and airplanes. Now the problem is that too many millions of Californians spill from the cities onto good farming land. The solution, up to now, has been to bulldoze the farm and import food from distant states to the east.

Though the population burgeons its millions more per decade and becomes increasingly a market for the state's produce, fewer and fewer citizens are willing to pick crops under traditional California conditions. As a result, California farm workers now lead America in trying to upgrade their lives, and farm owners lead America in trying to replace workers with machinery.

Nowhere have non-southern farmers more abused workers or resisted attempts to improve working conditions; yet nowhere else have farmers been quicker to run to federal and state agricultural agencies, especially the state university, to get socialized help in solving every sort of problem except the "labor problem."

In its way, California agriculture has made radical breaks with the past. Though farmers have been Republicans, and ever ready to rally to the cause of free enterprise, they have since the 1890s set precedents in forming co-operative water and irrigation systems and weather-predicting agencies. They have created scores of large and efficient co-operative marketing associations, dominated by the big growers and backed by state and federal laws on controlled marketing. Walnut growers made the trademark "Diamond" famous. Raisin growers established their "Sun Maid," and avocado raisers gave "Calavo" to the retail world. Prune and apricot people likewise pooled their efforts, as did almond growers, cattlemen, and others. The lemon and orange growers' exchanges merged into California Fruit Growers Exchange and later Sunkist Growers, Inc.; now the Sunkist teletype systems span the United States and Canada and link the principal markets of the globe.

During the first century of statehood California's agriculture was a biological triumph. Early explorers of the coasts and river valleys—Portola, Anza, Vancouver—saw much sand and rock, much seared grass and dry plain. But after heavy-eating gold seekers created a local consumers' market and the long railroads opened up the continent, Californians turned square miles of nondescript bottom and foothill land into cattle or sheep ranches, grain and vegetable fields, and vineyards and orchards. Scattered over a distance of 900 miles, favored spots became oases of almonds, figs, apricots, cherries, prunes, peaches, hops, oranges, lemons, English walnuts, celery, lettuce, wheat, barley, alfalfa, wine grapes. Individuals and government agents experimented endlessly with imported livestock, including camels and ostriches, and with plants from all the green continents.

There have been notable successes in adapting plants and their environment to each other, as, for example, dates, grapefruit and winter vegetables near Palm Springs; alfalfa, cantaloupe, and cattle feeding in the Imperial Valley; apple orchards along the coast near Monterey, Easter lilies along the extreme northwest coast, or rice on the hot plains alongside the upper Sacramento River. California developed the world capitals for lima beans, asparagus, figs and raisins, avocados. Portions of four Southern California counties became the Orange Empire. Coastal valleys produced more than half of the world's flower seeds.

This gigantic task in landscape architecture took place largely between 1870 and 1940. It turned entire flatland vistas, the flanks of long ranges, and vast blanched desert slopes into carefully tended open space. It was beautiful and enchanting; in the blossom seasons it was as fragrant as later it was profitable. Far from destroying natural beauty, most farmers had improved upon the original brush, flood plains and willow bottoms.

California, a leading commercial and industrial state, has balanced its economy by also being the leading agricultural state in value and variety of production. It grows commercially more than 200 crops, and ranks first in forty-three of them. The Experiment Station Extension Service calmly claims that California "productivity and variety [have] never been matched anywhere in the world's history."

In order to protect this gigantic "agribusiness," California guards its border like a military state, inspecting cars and trucks for pests. Inside the state, farmers and their advisers carry on a multifold biological, mechanical, and chemical war against more than 100 species of insects and mites (most of them as exotic as the crops they infest), plus many fungi and viruses, as well as gophers. In the nineteenth century, Californians pioneered in the use of benign insects to prey on harmful insects, as when they imported an Australian ladybird beetle to control the citrus-loving mealy bug. The more recent chemical war on pests, largely successful, though speeding up the evolution of resistant strains, is also highly effective in killing beneficial insects like bees, harmless birds, other wildlife and perhaps—slowly—human beings. The result, as Rachel Carson pointed out with California examples in *Silent Spring,* is a "web of death."

California is now also the country's leading automobile state, and the car is a special threat to its crops. Increasingly since around 1944, fumes from crankcases and exhaust pipes have created smog on sunny days, damaging alfalfa, cotton and grapes. In twenty years some ten different crops were driven out of the Los Angeles area. Spinach was the first to go, its leaves spoiled by brown spots and by bronzing or silvering on the lower sides. The same happened to celery, beets, mustard leaves, romaine lettuce, and other edible greens. Farmers, themselves prodigal users of cars and other gasoline-powered machines, face the prospect of joining the incipient revolt against the internal combustion engine.

In pilot social reform as in sheer gigantism of production, California agriculture is also showing the way. Growers now confront an economic revolution that they have long tried to prevent or delay. There is an unprecedented push to unionize hands in field and orchard and in packing sheds. After a century, farmers can foresee an end to their variation on the hacienda system of old Mexico. California's specialized farms have needed extra labor only during certain seasons. Since workers could not stay all year for a few months' work, they became migrants, falling into an itinerant annual cycle of subservience and exploitation, rootlessness, and misery.

After World War II, the *bracero* program, negotiated with Mexico, gave imported workers a basic and guaranteed standard of living and earning. Native workers did not come under this protection, and now that ethical and economic pressures have ended the *bracero* system, the archaic farm workers system is also ending. Professional farm workers, often Americans with Spanish names and Mexican or Filipino faces, are organizing, evolving to a new level of self-respect and of national concern.

The center of this movement for more than a year has been Delano, a small town in the lower San Joaquin Valley, where grape pickers went on strike in September, 1965. Their leader was a native American, Cesar Chavez, director of the National Farm Workers Association (NFWA). Backed by other AFL-CIO unions, by religious groups and liberals, opposed by millionaire owners and their small-town henchmen, the strike attracted international attention in the press and celebrated itself in a narrative account called *Huelga*. It ran a credit union, published a magazine, and supported a gay slapstick satirical troupe that put on skits in Spanish about landlords and the workers' problems.

Despite competition from the Teamsters' union, the NFWA astonished many when it signed an agreement with vineyards controlled by Schenley and won bargaining elections with the tough, recalcitrant, union-hating (but Teamster-preferring) Di Giorgio Corporation at ranches in Delano and Arvin.

Related to the development of farm workers' unions—making them possible and also perhaps making both unions and workers largely obsolete—is the new drive to mechanize agriculture. The machines invented to replace workers are designed at several branches of the University of California and in the shops of private engineers like those employed by Sunkist. Since their market at first is only in California, they do not attract national firms. They are manufactured by alert, small California firms such as Blackwelder of Rio Vista, Cochrane of Salinas, and Handling Equipment of Torrance.

The present technical development goes far beyond the earlier eastern inventions for harvesting grains and the early California concern with machines to level and work farm soils and to cut drainage or irrigation systems. The California challenge to engineers has not been hay or barley or cotton but specialties like carrots, melons, dates, lemons, celery, bell peppers, and oranges that take relatively huge amounts of hand labor. As this labor has become scarce or expensive or firmly self-respecting, the interlocking United States Department of Agriculture, California State Department of Agriculture and the university have set to work redesigning crops and inventing machinery to harvest them. Men are at work breeding asparagus, grapes, melons, even sesame seed that can be machine harvested. Tomato plants, the result of computer-controlled genetic breeding, have fruits of the same size, conveniently shaped, mostly ripening at the same time, and allegedly tasting like tomatoes; they can be picked all at once by a machine that pulls up the plant. Lettuce pickers that move as fast as a man can walk are equipped with pressure sensors to feel if a head is ready to pick, memory devices, and automatic knives to cut the stem. A cucumber machine carries pickers who ride stretched out on their stomachs above the equally prostrate vines.

To facilitate harvesting, fig, apple, peach, and lemon orchards have been pruned with low flat "plateau" tops, and costs of picking may soon lead to clipping the shapely rounded tops of orange trees to the dead level of butch haircuts. Indeed, citrus fruits, first and most famous of the California orchard bonanzas, have undergone the longest studies. These began in the 1890s with mechanical sorting, and have since included fruit washers, bulk handling in the orchard, natural coloring of fruits by use of ethylene, trademarking directly on each fruit, orchard heating on frosty nights, and systems planning of everything from placement of trees to layout in packing houses and warehouses. Instead of climbing a ladder, the picker rides in a cockpit on the end of a boom. He uses a push button to position himself. He picks an orange and deposits it in a tube that gently drops it to a box at the bottom of the machine. Studies are under way to devise machines for shaking citrus fruit off trees into canvas catchers, or for harvesting by means of an oscillating air blast.

More serious than the weather, the insects, the labor organizers, and the difficulties of mechanizing the harvest is the ominous urban growth. The very population that hungers for fresh produce threatens to crowd agriculture out of the state. At the moment, much farm activity survives only by escaping. Like the restless, ever-migrant population of California, agriculture is on the move. Whole dairies join the caravan, moving farther and farther away from the cities that use their milk and cottage cheese. Nurseries, their tons of portable trees in cans and barrels, take to the road in flight from shopping centers and apartment houses. While some crop specialties are certain to disappear, their unique soils smothered under jerry-built homes and shopping centers, other crops can make big jumps over mountain ranges to whole new watersheds.

In the old and famous parts of California, agriculture is being steadily paved or roofed over. The change in the areas surrounding Ventura and Los Angeles, San Jose and Santa Clara, Sacramento and San Diego is as visible and as significant as that from one geological epoch to another. Though minor California officials—experts—mutter now and then, there is no wide public concern over the destruction of the fertile oases of prime, unparalleled, irreplaceable land. The masses are too preoccupied with

bowling alleys, race tracks, and drive-in theatres to care about
the soil beneath the blacktop.

After World War II, Southern California began the ever more
rapid alteration of its landscape. Olives, muscat grapes, bee culture, and turkey raising were already centered in Northern California; now from the broad sweep of established agriculture south
of the Tehachapi Mountains, Southern California specialties began
to depart for the eastern deserts or for the northern valleys, where
walnuts, head lettuce, olives, celery, artichokes, and dairying developed new production enclaves.

During and after World War II, as millions arrived to make
ships and planes or to ride them off to the wars, the trend to put
homes and factories on farmland took over in Northern California
as well. This time there were fewer opportunities for agriculture
to move. Though government at all levels began to tinker with
zoning and planning, it made no plans for agriculture. For the
building and loan companies, the mortgage companies, the big
real estate operators (often Easterners), the contractors with their
fleets of bulldozers and other earth-moving apparatus, the state
highway engineers (who hate trees, dislike curves, and shudder
at the word *beauty*), and allied county supervisors and state legislators—for all those who profited from "Progress," the rancher
and farmer were like the Indian of yore. They were wasters of
open space. Sound investment, the needs of a forward-looking
population, GNP, and other mystical phrases called for action:
they turned orchards and fields, flower-seed farms, feed lots and
dairy barns, range land, and forests of second-growth timber into
housing tracts, new towns, freeways, airfields, reservoirs, drive-in
churches, department stores, amusement parks, factories, warehouses, junk yards, military camps, missile bases, golf links
(themselves vulnerable to apartment house builders), and parking lots for square miles of motionless motor vehicles.

These new space users, said to be good economics, were created
at a heavy cost in scenery and environment, regional flavor, and

local identity. The new users threatened the balance of the state's economy, for a state without agriculture is badly off. Prices of fruits, vegetables and milk went up. Flavorsome California oranges became so expensive that the oncoming generations came to prefer frozen orange concentrate, relatively tasteless, from out of state.

In the late 1950s, men began to foresee the end of agriculture in the most productive parts of California. Bulldozers were uprooting orange trees at the rate of one every fifty-five seconds. Of these, countless thousands each week were in Los Angeles County, where for a time earth-moving machinery destroyed 3,000 acres of orange orchard a day.

It was not only citrus trees that lost their hold on the earth. Bulldozers shoved out prime apricot orchards in Hemet Valley, chicken farms in Arcadia, hop fields in the American River bottom land near Sacramento, spinach and onions on the Santa Maria plain, lima beans in Oxnard, olive groves in San Fernando Valley, where the 2,000-acre grove at Sylmar had been "the largest single olive grove in the world." The stately palms were felled in the Indio date gardens, where soils and trees alike represented a half-century of ingenuity, to make way for motels and tracts of trailers. The big shovels ripped into avocado orchards on the hills of Fallbrook and Vista, a region designed by destiny for raising the fruit delicacy. Housing contractors, or highway builders, or both, hacked into pear orchards on fabulous soil south of Clear Lake and into grapevines of what once was "the globe's largest vineyard," an inspiring panorama on the sandy alluvial fans of Cucamonga. The slopes between Stanford University (once lovingly called "The Farm") and San Jose, which in 1940 were a modern Eden of orchards and truck gardens, got roofed over into a routine patchwork suburbia.

In 1963, California was converting 375 acres of agricultural land a day to meet the urban needs of newcomers. Most of these acres were from the one-sixth of the state that is relatively good soil. A million acres of prime soil have been lost since 1945 and many more will be lost, as things are going. A few years ago the Governor's Advisory Committee on Housing saw the population as doubling by 1980, with the state then 90 per cent urbanized. A private housing expert has predicted that in the next fifteen years Californians will build as many new houses as they built between the time of the first Spanish adobe and today.

Americans face no foreseeable famine, no shortages of calories. They can always eat wheat, corn, soy beans, beef, and eggs. But they may well have to forget the delights of California oranges, table grapes, wines, walnuts, winter peas, early melons, and fall raspberries. Gone perhaps will be crops that Americans grow only in California: Persian melons, avocados, persimmons, artichokes, almonds, figs, garlic, nectarines, olives, pomegranates, and certain de luxe dates that grow below sea level near Thermal.

Grave concern over the loss of farm land to subdivisions and industrial and military uses has stimulated radical proposals for salvation—California pioneers in cures as in catastrophes. One device used by farmers to save their occupations from city people has been to incorporate their lands to form "cities"—Dairy Valley, to save milk farms, or Fremont, to save orchards. But a basic problem has been a constitutional provision that county assessors must value all land for tax purposes on the basis of "the highest and best use"—a rule that dooms a cauliflower field if a "de luxe" housing tract goes up next to it. Thanks to leapfrog and "scatteration" developments, many farmers have had their taxes suddenly spurt up above their income from the land. One Sacramento almond grower had a 2,446 per cent tax increase in one year.

In 1966, the voters passed an amendment that bases assessments and taxes for open space on actual use, not on development potential. This welcome step had been anticipated by the legislature a year before in the California Land Conservation Act, designed to create agricultural "preserves," analogous to the wilderness areas established elsewhere in the country. These are set up by contracts between farmers and local governments, with tax concessions for continuing to farm. The Act of 1965 and the Amendment of 1966 assert that California's cities should grow solid, concentrate, and mature, instead of impetuously racing out on all sides, putting up buildings at random, leaving no rural sweep of scene. The laws imply that taxation is not just a way to raise money; it is also an expression of public policy.

The 1966 Amendment, if properly implemented by legislative action, will greatly help Californians to retain the nonurban landscape that still remains. The legislature will bear close watching, and this will be done by enlightened farming interests, including some big old ranches, and by new nonprofit organizations, bright, alert, properly aggressive, such as California Tomorrow, with its quarterly *Cry California,* and the Planning and Conservation League for Legislative Action, which keeps a full-time lobbyist in Sacramento.

The one over all cure for the loss of agricultural domain is statewide planning, administered by a state commission as removed from monetary pressures and politics as is the state supreme court. Such a body could apply suggestions such as those in the report on open spaces made by the landscape architects firm of Eckbo, Dean, Austin and Williams, of whom the State Office of Planning requested "truly bold proposals." The report, full of new legal, fiscal, and ideological concepts, is part of the State Development Plan, years in preparation, which considers agricultural and other open space, as well as cities, fish and game, and varied amenities. The plan, pushed by the forward-looking Edmund Brown administration, has dropped out of sight under Brown's successor, Ronald Reagan, well publicized as a private land speculator and an "economy-minded" governor. Meanwhile the pressures grow that will force California to move on with planning a program that assures agriculture and every other broad life-sustaining value a due and permanent place under the California sun.

The program will involve the old idea, long forgotten, now revolutionary again, that private ownership of land has narrow limits, that it is only a license to use land or water surface. This license is granted by society on the understanding that certain rules are obeyed and certain fees (called taxes) are regularly paid, also provided that society does not have a higher use for the land and water. Many arrangements are possible: eminent domain proceedings, followed by restricted leasebacks; purchase by the state of certain rights; contractual arrangements prohibiting urbanization, with either the state or the individual owning the fee simple. The basic idea is that we need a new land ethic: it must become illegal to destroy beauty, violate ecology, smash history—to extinguish the natural things that give value to human life.

Anyone who views the present chaotic surface of the state may find it hard to believe that California will—soon enough—create an all-powerful state planning commission. But then it is also hard to believe that Californians will let their agriculture, like their scenery, like their clean sea water and clear atmosphere, pass into oblivion. Unless the state has changed utterly from what it was in the past, answers will come out of California as the pinch, already felt, becomes an ultimatum. The state that has led the way in crop production, co-operative selling, unionization of grape pickers, mechanization of orchards, and calculated destruction of agricultural marvels can also lead the way in planning.

California can do whatever it wants. It can use its mountains to fill in San Francisco Bay and the ocean above the continental shelf and there build more suburbs and parking lots. It can exterminate any and all species of birds, mammals, and plants. Or it can restrict or ban the car, the bulldozer, the subdivider, and the speculator. It can save or reconstitute much of its agriculture, as it can much of its shore line and mountain back country. Salvation is as possible as destruction.

Howard F. Gregor

WATER AND THE
CALIFORNIA PARADOX

Alone of the heavily populated states in the Union, California has its population concentrated in semiarid and arid areas. Yet population increase has been greater here than in other states and agricultural production has achieved a premier position. This sharp contradiction between intense human activity and deficient rainfall is the ultimate tribute to the success of Californians in obtaining enough water. But progress has also brought problems which have grown more complicated as reclamation efforts have increased. As water supplies decrease in the humid areas, and as populations press more closely on the margins of the dry lands, how Californians meet these problems will be increasingly scrutinized.

The preference of people for the drier parts of the state is not new in California history. Spaniards established missions along

159

the drier central and southern coasts, and not in the wetter lowlands of the northern coast, the mountains, and in the Sierra Nevada foothills, where large streams abound. With the arrival of
the Americans, the disparity between population and humid area
increased. Although the Gold Rush briefly made the Sierra foothills the principal population center of the state, people soon
began to abandon the mines and to swell the population of San
Francisco. But already as early as 1870, the growth rate of Los
Angeles had begun to exceed that of the Bay city. Shortly after
1920, Los Angeles became the largest city of California. Since
1940, the population supremacy of southern, and drier, California has been dramatically reinforced. Population doubled from
1940 to 1960, giving that region for the first time over half (57
per cent) of the total state number. The gain also almost equaled
the entire San Francisco Bay Area population for 1960. Total
population in southern California for 1960 exceeded 9 million
and was expected to reach at least 16 million by 1980.

Rural population also has displayed an early and increasing
gravitation to the drier lands. Gold mining stimulated the first
serious agricultural activity in the Sacramento Valley and the Bay
Area, but by the 1870s farming had begun to spread into the semiarid and arid San Joaquin Valley. Also by this time agriculture
was beginning on a large scale in coastal southern California.
Farmers began to move into the arid Imperial Valley in larger
numbers after 1900, and, more recently, into the drier west side
of the San Joaquin Valley.

The preference by Californians for drier areas is not illogical.
As in most of the West, the sections that receive most of the pre-
cipitation are also the least fitted for cultivation. Mountain and
hill lands force air to rise and cool and condense, but this is of
little comfort to one who wants to farm in the area. Growing seasons are also cooler and shorter in the highlands and soils are
thinner or nonexistent. For better growing conditions, then, one
must go to the lower, and drier, basins and plains. And these are

abundant in central and southern California. Moreover these low lands have physical advantages over much of the rest of American farm land. Aridity may make for a water problem, but it also discourages plant diseases and weeds, reduces soil erosion, facilitates drying of fruit, and, with high temperatures and an abundance of sunshine, promotes huge yields per acre. Farm machinery also encounters little resistance on a terrain that in much of these lowlands is suggestive of the Great Plains.

Most Californians, however, being urban dwellers, have undoubtedly been attracted even more by the aridity. Rain, and even snow to a degree, may be good for crops, but they are of no help to the "patio living" that appeals to so many California urbanites. Economic attractions of the growing cities, as well as their cultural advantages, have reinforced this climatic pull, until now it has become difficult to decide which stimulus is currently the most powerful in the California migration. Undoubtedly the rising level of prosperity throughout the country has made it easier for people to choose an area for its pleasant living conditions rather than just for a job. They form a new kind of migrant in the history of population movements, and California has become one of the few areas in the world to receive them in quantity. Certainly nowhere else in the United States has our proverbial search for the "good life" had such implications for the water resource as in California.

The surge of people into the drier parts of California has been closely supported by an equally stormy advance in hydraulic technology. Fortunately, the state has a rich watershed in its northern mountains, as well as the Colorado River on its southeastern corner. A great part of the reclamation effort, therefore, has concentrated on transporting this water to the areas of need. The welter of pipelines, dams, reservoirs, canals, pumping plants, and power plants today reflect the vigor and success of this effort. They are also, however, an evidence of constantly increasing need, for achievements in hydraulic technology, coupled with economic and other forces, have fostered a cycle of population growth that now makes the water situation in California more critical than ever.

Probably in no other place has this been so evident as in Los Angeles, a prime example of a metropolitan center born of modern hydraulic technology. In 1907, the city began construction of an aqueduct to tap the Owens River on the eastern side of the Sierra Nevada, 240 miles away. Completed in 1915, the aqueduct was already deemed insufficient two years later. It was therefore extended 100 miles farther north to the vicinity of Mono Lake, necessitating a boring through volcanic cones for part of the line. But by 1931, the water situation in southern California had worsened to the point where Los Angeles and twelve other cities voted bonds to construct another aqueduct, this time to the Colorado River. It was completed in 1941, the aqueduct now bringing Colorado River water over a 400-mile route to Los Angeles. Water for the line was stored behind the then tallest dam in the United States, Hoover (then Boulder) Dam. The reservoir, Lake Mead, was also the largest of its kind in the world. The entire project proved to be the forerunner of TVA, Grand Coulee, and other multiple-purpose projects subsequently built. This was also the project that was to ensure a safe water supply for Los Angeles until at least 1980. But then came World War II and still another surge of population. A parallel Owens-Mono aqueduct has now been completed, but the city still anxiously awaits water from the Feather River Project, a reclamation scheme that will bring water from the northern Sierras, almost 700 miles away. Oroville Dam, the key control structure in the scheme, was completed in 1967. Its height of 735 feet tops that of Hoover Dam, and makes it the highest earthen dam in the world. The aqueduct is expected to reach Los Angeles in 1972, precisely when the water situation is again expected to become critical. Then another breathing space until the 1990s is expected.

The San Francisco Bay Area urban agglomeration has had a similar history of water-supply development. By 1930, the city of San Francisco had acquired water sources in the southern part of the San Francisco Peninsula and in the hills east of San Francisco Bay. Then in 1934 the city built an aqueduct to the Sierra Nevada. Two lines now bring water to the city and reservoir facilities continue to be expanded. The East Bay cities, including Oakland, Berkeley, and Alameda, tapped the Sierra even earlier, in 1929. A second and paralleling aqueduct was built in 1949, and a third was finished in 1963. On the southern end of San Francisco Bay, rapidly growing San Jose and its neighboring cities wait for additional water to be provided by a branch aqueduct of the Feather River Project.

California farmers have also shared in this interplay of technological advance and increased demand, although the race between the two developments has been a more recent happening. Irrigators at first used only surface water, and it was not until they tapped underground supplies extensively that irrigation farming began to expand significantly. Now deep-well turbine pumps plumb depths of hundreds to thousands of feet. Hydroelectricity, developed by the many water projects, powers the pumps, and helps to explain why more than 96 per cent of California farms are electrified. This is easily the highest rate of farm electrification in the country. Sprinkler irrigation systems have become especially popular since World War II with the introduction of improvements such as quick coupling and aluminum tubing. Sprinklers are far more efficient than furrows, and, by eliminating the need for preliminary leveling, have made possible irrigation of terrain formerly considered too rough for intensive agricultural development.

But most important since World War II has been the increasing dependence on importation of water. Since the late 1940s the overwhelming share of new irrigation supplies has come from the Central Valley Project, a reclamation scheme much more complex than the TVA or Grand Coulee and only now to be surpassed in size by the Feather River Project. The CVP is designed to accomplish all of the objectives associated with a complete multiple-purpose project: expansion of irrigation and domestic water supplies, production of power, prevention of floods, improvement of navigation, and provision of recreational facilities. Irrigation expansion has been the primary purpose, however, with the CVP facilities being planned for diverting surplus water from the Sacramento Valley to the drier, but also larger and warmer, San Joaquin Valley to the south. Although still not fully completed, the project already deserves a large share of the credit for California's leading position in agricultural production. Farm production value in the San Joaquin Valley alone now surpasses that of forty-four states.

Yet irrigation farming has always been expensive, and, as expenses have risen, the urge for still more irrigation simply to meet costs rather than make profits has increased. New means of extracting water from underground sources have also encouraged faster-falling water tables, which, in turn, can only be remedied by more wells, more pumps, and pumps that go to greater depths. Thus, for example, cotton farmers on the western side of the San Joaquin Valley must irrigate throughout the year in order to amortize their investment in turbine pumps, even though cotton is raised for only part of the year. Also, more land than just that occupied by cotton is needed for this additional irrigation, since the other crops grown are winter grains which use only one-fourth the water needed by cotton.

Salinification control has become still another growing financial liability to the irrigator as he has expanded his facilities. Movement of ground water upward into the drier surface layers of the soil is common in dry lands, and addition of irrigation water, particularly in a wasteful way, greatly accelerates the process. Unfortunately, the salts that collect in large amounts in dry land soils are also partly dissolved by the water and carried to the surface. There they poison the root zone or, if concentrated enough, even form a hardpan impermeable to root penetration. Then the only remedy is to flush out the salts, but this requires large additional amounts of water and an extensive drainage system. Already thousands of miles of drainage ditches and tile pipes underlie California farm lands and a "master drain" for the San Joaquin Valley has been proposed.

Just the fact that present and future irrigation projects are bound to extend the irrigated zones is still another guarantee of an increasingly expensive irrigation economy. Sixty per cent of the potentially irrigable land in California (and 37 per cent of that in western United States) lies in the San Joaquin Valley and the southeastern desert region. Yet little of this land is as good as that now irrigated. Water levels are lower in both areas and boron degrades soil quality in the San Joaquin Valley. In the desert, soils are less retentive of water and the best types are widely dispersed and fragmented in their distribution. To make such areas yield as much as the older and better irrigated lands will obviously require a much higher investment.

That many farmers are failing to keep pace with their neighbors in meeting the rapidly rising costs of what is already an expensive and exacting type of farming can be seen in the declining number of farms and the enlargement of those remaining. This is still more evidence of the growing nationwide contradiction between our traditional belief in the right of a man to own a farm and the increasingly large scale of operations needed to meet farming expenses. In no other state, however, is this social-economic conflict so stark as in California. On the one side is a farming economy in which the "industrial farm" has been a major part of California agriculture almost from the beginning and today has reached its peak of success in that state; on the other side is the most determined effort by the federal government to date to keep farms small and thus available to more people. This effort is based on the Reclamation Act of 1902, which requires that landowners on all projects undertaken by the Bureau of Reclamation sell holdings in excess of 160 acres (or, as construed under the community property laws of California, 320 acres). If the landowner wants project water for his excess holdings, he must enter into a contract with the Bureau to sell his excess lands within ten years of the contract signing. Such an action was carried out for the first time in 1964, when the Bureau broke up a seven-million-dollar farm of the Di Giorgio Corporation into 160-acre parcels for auction. Only one buyer bid, and in a second auction in 1965, only two made an offer. They deposited 10 per cent of a total price of $548,500 for 300 acres. The customers were a president of a San Francisco shipping firm and his wife. That these meager responses may have helped to bring about a historic reappraisal of government land policy is seen in the recent request by the Federal Reclamation Commissioner for Congress to take "a good hard look" at the acreage limitation applying to reclamation projects.

Increasingly high costs of California irrigation farming also are closely related to the accelerating competition between farmers and cities for water. That most major water projects in the last thirty years, excepting the Central Valley Project, have been initiated by, and constructed for use by urban areas emphasizes the growing dominance of cities in water control. It also shows that even if 90 per cent of the water used in California is still used for irrigation, most of the capital needed for future land reclamation projects will have to come from urban centers. And this financial control will obviously increase as urban populations expand, project sites become more difficult, and projects become larger. Combined with capital control is also the growing political power of the cities.

The Feather River Project is the best instance to date of the effect of this growing twofold dominance. Final approval of the project was delayed for several years by both the legislature and the Metropolitan Water District of Southern California until a firm guarantee of a permanent supply of water was made to that region. This, despite the immediate concern of Central Valley farmers over a falling water table and the fact that this region would be allocated 60 per cent of the water provided by the project.

Rapid urban expansion over adjacent agricultural lands has further weakened the rural side in water competition and also worsened the water situation in general. For the farmers, the widely dispersed pattern of urban growth often means an abrupt termination of operations by the disruption of irrigation and drainage lines. Otherwise, intensification is resorted to as rising land values and assessment rates herald the approach of the city. One of the principal means of intensification is the planting of more truck crops. They meet the growing market demands admirably and their short growing period enables the farmer to plant several successive crops during the long growing season. They also allow him to use the many and irregularly-shaped plots left in the wake of urban advance. But the tenderness and shallow roots of truck crops and their numerous plantings make them heavy water users. This need for moisture is also greatest in the summer when the water table is lowest.

Water demands increase even more drastically as the city finally takes over the land. At one time, a block of homes used only the same amount of water as a block of irrigated land, but dishwashers, garbage disposals, and more watering of lawns and plants are now steadily altering the ratio. In addition, cementing and sewering of surfaces reduces the chance of water reuse. Former rural land is also compacted, thus decreasing the capacity of the underground reservoirs and increasing the winter runoff, from which California gets the largest part of its water.

Little would seem to indicate that California farmers will find any relief from the growing pressure of the cities on present and future water supplies. Desalinization of sea water could perhaps eventually completely supply the cities, leaving the water of the Sierra Nevada and the Colorado River for the agricultural regions. But costs of desalinization and of the power that would be needed to pump the reclaimed water from the coast are still well above what can be met by urban populations. Moreover, there is also the probability that California agriculture will by that time have already found its limits, not in a dearth of water but in a lack of land. As early as 1950, a Stanford University report on national water resources policy was recommending that priority in all future water reclamation schemes in California and the rest of the West should be given to urban uses, while the East with its surplus of water could satisfy the increased food demands of the West, if needed. This would reverse the historical economic sequence in dry lands, in which irrigation has preceded other water uses.

Still it is hard to see how such a solution would not drastically reduce the nation's productive capacity, particularly in a period of changing diets and rapidly growing populations, both at home and overseas. California now supplies the nation with almost half of its fruits and nuts, a third of its vegetables, and a tenth of its field crops. Also, a goodly number of the crops raised in California cannot be produced elsewhere in the country because of certain strict physical requirements for growth. That the majority of Californians recognize this tremendous productivity was evidenced by the passing in 1965 of the California Land Conservation Act, which allows a city or county to enter into agreements with landowners for the purpose of preserving prime agricultural land. Just how successful the Act will be remains to be seen.

The most fundamental conflict between water users, though, stems from a lack of agreement between the boundaries of political units and those of hydrographic basins. It is an irony of the first order that in the West, where the richly watered areas are few and dispersed and rivers are often the only carriers of moisture over distances of hundreds of miles, boundaries have been drawn the most arbitrarily. Either they cut across basins and prevent a co-ordinated development of the natural unity, or they cut off the wetter basins from those that are in greater need of moisture. Both discordancies have helped make the constant search for water in California also one of almost constant regional strife.

The urban fragmentation of the Los Angeles Basin long worked to the advantage of Los Angeles because of its greater capital resources and better access to water sources. As water supplies worsened, the smaller, adjacent cities were faced with the alternatives of stagnation or getting additional water from Los Angeles at the price of annexation. Dry cycles were followed regularly by new surges in Los Angeles areal and population growth. But as Los Angeles began to eye the Colorado River for additional water, discretion tempered aggressiveness and the city joined with several others in southern California to ensure sufficient capital for the Colorado River Project. The product of this co-operation, the Metropolitan Water District of Southern California, now comprises almost a hundred cities, with a population of over eight million people and a total investment exceeding $400 million.

County boundaries have contributed to an even greater obstacle to co-ordinated planning for water reclamation, the historic rivalry of wetter northern and drier southern California. Northern California has long recognized its vulnerable position of greater water supplies but smaller population in relation to southern California, and has depended on the State Senate to protect it from any water projects that might, in its opinion, cripple its own growth. With the Senate represented on a county basis and with over three-quarters of the counties in northern California, one can well understand the heated opposition of many in this region to the Supreme Court's application of the "one man, one vote" principle to both state legislative houses. However, the areal contradiction of water and need is also increasing for urban and agricultural interests in the drier parts of northern California, and this probably played some part in the recent approval of legislative reapportionment. Certainly it contributed to the approval of the

Feather River Project, which, besides helping southern California, will also bring large amounts of water to both the Bay Area urban complex and Central Valley farm lands.

Reapportionment does not apply to the problem of interstate rivalries in water development, however, and in this most Californians might heartily wish for reapportionment of the federal Senate. Since most of the suitable sites for large multiple-purpose projects within the state are already fully developed, and even larger projects will be the order of the future, California can only hope for federal support. This support, in turn, hinges on the co-operation of other western states, which have few congressmen but many senators. Their number has often ensured more conflict than co-operation among the states sharing the Colorado River Basin. Only a 1963 United States Supreme Court decision was able to end a forty-year battle between Arizona and California over allocation of Colorado water. And, only in 1965 did the discrepancy between water reserves and booming demand become serious enough to induce all basin states to agree on an overall development of the Colorado River in the form of the 1.7-billion-dollar Colorado River Basin Project. But the agreement simply transfers the problem to a larger theater since the upper Colorado Basin states made their co-operation contingent on the execution of studies on the feasibility of importing water from the Columbia River Basin. A project linking the power lines of Bonneville and Hoover dams has now been approved by Congress, although Pacific Northwest states are still highly chary of any proposals for exporting Columbia water. That reluctance and the recent conservationist opposition to proposed dams on the Colorado have now at least delayed legislation on the Basin Project.

Meanwhile some thoughts are already turning to possibilities of transporting vast amounts of water and power over international boundaries. A Los Angeles engineering firm has proposed a project, labeled the North American Water and Power Alliance (NAWAPA), in which water would be sent from Alaska and northwestern Canada to the Canadian Prairies, the American West, and Mexico. The complexities in international relations and sectional rivalries that such a plan might present are endless. Yet just the fact that a private firm felt it worthwhile to spend five years in developing the plan would seem to reflect a growing general conviction that increasing water needs will eventually overcome regional antagonisms. This has been the lesson of the past, and there seems no reason why events in California and the West should not again confirm it. Its confirmation, however, may well have results unequaled in reclamation history.

13

Gladwin Hill

CALIFORNIA POLITICS

California's surprising choice of an actor to be its governor is the latest of a long series of events down the decades that have caused people everywhere to ask: "Isn't there something intrinsically extraordinary about California politics?"

A rococo kaleidescope of anomalies comes to mind: the belated California vote in 1916 that swung the Presidency from Hughes to Wilson . . . the tragi-comic regime of Governor "Sunny Jim" Rolph, who condoned a lynching, sent whiskey to a condemned man in San Quentin, and, at the bottom of the Depression, proposed that everybody just take a week's holiday . . . the vertiginous days of Upton Sinclair's EPIC campaign . . . the 600,000 votes cast, at the peak of the recent Red-baiting era, for a candidate for state superintendent of education who was an avowed Communist. . . .

James Bryce, the loftiest political analyst of modern times, summed it up crisply many years ago: "The politics of Cali-

fornia," he said, "is unique." Subsequent events have done nothing
but fortify this judgment.

Why *are* (to take a syntactical liberty with Professor Bryce) the
politics of California unique?

There is a great cat's-cradle of reasons. But it begins, inevitably, with *people*. It's people, after all, who make politics.

Every week there are more than 6,000 new and additional Californians who weren't there the week before. The rest of the country probably has gotten tired of hearing about this. It sounds like
chamber of commerce talk. Even Californians get tired of hearing
about it. But, intriguing or tiresome, it's a fact that can't be
begged in any consideration of Californians' unpredictable and
often curious political behavior.

For the last hundred years, year in and year out, month in and
month out, week in and week out—while the Civil War was
fought, the Spanish-American War, and two World Wars; while
motion pictures and aviation grew from unknowns into major
industries; while the dusty pueblo of Los Angeles was burgeoning
into the nation's second largest metropolis—California has experienced a population growth averaging 3,000 souls a week. More
than half this increase has been from immigration, as opposed to
indigenous multiplication—probably the most prolonged and massive migration in the world's history.

The continuing nature of the influx is indicated in the fact that
of California's last half-dozen governors, only two have been native
Californians; the present one was born in Illinois.

The political impact of this steady population rise is intimated
in the fact that in 1966 the electorate of some 8,000,000 contained
nearly 1,000,000 persons who were not qualified voters in the
preceding state election in 1962.

Today around 60 per cent of California's population still consists of people from somewhere else. They have come from all
the other forty-nine states in rough proportion to their sizes, as
well as from foreign countries. To a degree they form a cross

section of the United States. This is reflected, probably, in the fact that California's choice for President has usually concurred with the nation's choice; in this century there have been only two hairline exceptions, when two native sons, Governor Hiram Johnson (1912) and Richard Nixon (1960) were on the losing national ticket.

But a geographical cross section does not mean a mental and emotional cross section. The typical Marylander, after all, is not someone who leaves Maryland to go to California. Geographically and in other aspects, California has long been the last frontier. Frontiers historically attract two sorts of people, the enterprising and adventurous, and the escapists—in both cases, rugged individualists.

From Leland Stanford, the sanctimonious railroad pirate-cum-governor, to Los Angeles' erstwhile Mayor Norris Poulson—who horrified the State Department by rhetorically spitting in Premier Khrushchev's eye—California's development is a story of individualists with a blithe disregard for conventions and norms—and a populace that has consistently given individualists moral support. This atmosphere of laissez faire is as distinctive as California's climate, and newcomers are quickly enveloped in it.

When asked to function, as in presidential elections, as a unit of the United States, Californians defer to prevailing criteria. But when called upon to shape their internal politics, they have always said in effect: "We'll tailor them to suit ourselves."

California's home-grown brand of politics has gone far toward rejecting the hallowed two-party system. Outward forms have been deceptively preserved, as a sort of public security-blanket. But behind this false front reigns a politics of pragratism. In effect, each election time, Californians look around and see how conditions in their state are. Then they look around, almost casually, to assess the most palatable people in sight to do the work for another four years.

No compulsion is felt to maintain continuity in the political apparatus. Systematic development of political timber is an exercise in which the hoarier states may indulge; in California that's tacitly classified as cheating—something that would take the fun, the spontaneity, the pragmatism, out of the game.

The party label a candidate wears doesn't make so much difference. Until 1959, he could compete in as many different primaries as he wanted, in effect masquerading as a member of each party whose nomination he sought. Party organizations are forbidden by law to indicate any preference for one primary aspirant over another: a man who has served ably in public office for twenty years is not differentiated on the ballot, except for his occupational designation, from a world-is-flat eccentric who has just come out of the woodwork and put down the nominal filing fee.

Formalized ideology is not of much account. Californians select party candidates in June; it's only in August that the parties, to comply with the law, meet fleetingly and propound platforms, which by that time neither candidates nor voters are disposed to pay much attention to.

Then comes a whirlwind propaganda campaign, with emphasis on the professional image-makers, the television, radio, and billboard time-and-space buyers, the mimeograph crankers.

With voter attachments so loose and imponderable, a candidate would be foolish to make a party-line appeal. He must, for safety, woo both Republicans and Democrats. He must probe for issues that cut across party lines, but are calculated to polarize a decisive flock of voters—a flamboyant pension plan, the open-shop question, an appeal to sectional or racial prejudice, or in the final extremity, fearless advocacy of uncontroversial boons like better highways and lower taxes. Ronald Reagan even extolled "morality," although without more explicit definition its political meaning is elusive.

As chaotic and unreasonable as it all sounds, the system has redeeming features. The over-Niagara-Falls-in-a-barrel competition does tend to separate men from boys, to put a premium on the best organizers and shrewdest strategists. Even in a mad poker game with half the cards wild, superior players tend to come out ahead. It's the obverse of the traditional system in which inferior individuals can coast into office shrouded in the panoply of party, and serve in the format of "party responsibility" which may be efficient or inefficient, honest or corrupt.

The urge to pragmatism appeared in California as soon as the Forty-Niners.

The nascent state's very first political rally, a gathering in San Francisco, October 25, 1849, of nominal Democrats, prophetically propounded the ringing declaration: "Partyism for the sake of party merely, we totally reject."

The expression was not just a passing whim. By 1873, the pragmatic spirit had crystallized into a "People's Independent Party," whose convention declared:

> One of the most serious obstacles in the way of political and governmental reform lies in the doctrine of so-called 'party fealty,' that tyrannical rule which degrades the citizen and sinks him to the servile partisan, rendering him the helpless tool of selfish wire-pullers and caucus-manipulators . . . We hold that any citizen has the right to take part in good faith in the actions and deliberations of any political organization, caucus or convention, without being bound thereby except so far as his own judgment and conscience may approve.

The People's Independent Party, like many in the state's turbulent history, was short-lived. But its sentiments gathered impetus under other labels as the decades went by.

The endless tide of migration made the California populace intrinsically unstable. An idea had little chance to take root before there was another freshet of newcomers ready with variations. Seventy-six thousand Californians voted in the presidential election

of 1852; 97,000 four years later; 155,000 in 1876; nearly 200,-
000 in 1884.

Geography militated against conventional political cohesion.
California's inhabitants were scattered over a north-south expanse
of nearly 1,000 miles; its two main concentrations of population,
in an era of horse transportation, were 500 miles apart. In 1859,
the two sections agreed to form separate states, and only Congress's preoccupation with the impending Civil War prevented
the split from being ratified. It still was being advocated as late
as 1880. A century later this sectionalism is cemented into laws
prescribing northern and southern divisions for the major political
parties, and apportioning major state subventions on a north-south
basis.

In California's first half-century its ever-growing citizenry was
preoccupied with carving utopia out of the wilderness—construct-
ing roads, extracting minerals, irrigating the deserts, developing
agriculture and industry toward their present remarkable levels.

Once the Civil War was past and the slavery issue settled, the
reigning problems perennially were *non-partisan* problems—fighting Indians, balancing the state's perpetually queasy budget,
providing institutions for malefactors and unfortunates. For a
generation, two of the most burning issues were Chinese immigration (a perpetual scapegoat for everyone's frustrations) and
labor's struggle for organization and amenities. On both of these,
the major parties tended less to take opposing stands than to differ
only in fluctuating emphasis.

The supercharged atmosphere of dynamism and change played
a reciprocal cause-and-effect role in radicalism on both the right
and the left. The pendulum swung from the Vigilantes and
Know-Nothings of the 1850s to Dennis Kearney's axe-handle-
wielding Workingmen's Party in the 1870s; from the Sinclairism
of the 1930s to Birchism and Goldwaterism in the 1960s.

A popular irreverence for elected officials was reflected in a
cavalier disregard for continuity of administration; it was extraor-

dinary if a governor who had served four years was accorded
even his party's renomination, and, up to 1914, none was ever
re-elected.

In this atmosphere of bemusement, preoccupation, and splinter
fanaticism, "The Octopus" immortalized by Frank Norris, the
Southern Pacific Railroad, quickly consolidated its historic
stranglehold on the political and economic life of California.
Playing Machiavellian politics all the way from crossroads to the
halls of Congress—and viewing the two parties only as mechanisms
to be played off against each other—the amoral corporate colossus
built by Stanford, Huntington, Crocker, and Hopkins bribed and
pressured its way into such outrageous dominance that it finally
collapsed under its own weight.

When the crest of the national reform wave hit California in
1910, the two political parties used almost identical language in
declaring that the Southern Pacific must be exorcised root and
branch from its ubiquitous encroachments on the public's
prerogatives.

As standard bearer for the reform crusade, Governor Hiram
Johnson propounded the thesis that since the Southern Pacific's
awful domination had been effected through the apparatus of
political parties, the remedy was to smash that apparatus. And
that is what was done, with ingenuity that matched the SP's
political perversions.

The cohesion essential to any political party was vitiated—
first by making all city and county politics non-partisan, eliminating the basic building blocks of organization politics; and insti-
tuting a thoroughgoing civil service merit system, which mini-
mized patronage.

But just in case there should be any residual organizational
vitality, two more crushing blows were dealt. The legal specifica-
tions of party organizations were altered to exclude local and
county units from participation in the statewide party committees.
And cross-filing was instituted—turning primaries into free-for-alls
and making party-line voting as difficult as possible.

To cap all else, the Johnson regime introduced the initiative, the referendum and recall, which meant that citizens could instigate legislation, second-guess their legislators, or fire any official from governor to school board, with no reference to party structures.

The innovations so blurred party lines that even though from 1934 on the Republicans were an ever-growing minority in registration, they continued to run the state over most of the next quarter-century, essentially by sheer momentum.

The Progressive-reformist "nonpartisanism" that Hiram Johnson expounded seemed to wane and wither in the quarter-century after he went to the United States Senate in 1917. Upton Sinclair's abortive utopianism in the Depression era precipitated a reprise of McKinley Republicanism in the governorship of Frank Merriam (1934–38); and the anachronistic inadequacy of this swung the electorate the other way, to the choice of Culbert Olson, the only Democratic governor in forty years.

But then came Earl Warren, who expounded bipartisan "nonpartisanism" in a modern dimension Hiram Johnson could hardly have dreamed of. In 1946, Warren won both parties' nomination for re-election, a feat achieved by no other governor before or since. The century-old philosophy that "California problems transcend party lines" was resuscitated with such vigor that it set the stage for the Democratic comeback of 1958, with Governor Brown's election, and was an indispensable keynote of the 1966 Reagan campaign.

Cross-filing became such a confusing nuisance that the legislature revoked it in 1959 and California returned to conventional primaries. But with all the other factors militating against party regularity, the change hasn't made much difference.

Party organizations are essentially mailing addresses and skeletal structures in which a small coterie of activists indulge in factional jousting. When asked, after the 1966 election, who might assume titular leadership of the defeated Democrats, the party's foremost "professional," Assembly Speaker Jesse Unruh, said he didn't think there really was much for anyone to lead—that California parties were less coherent entities than transitory assortments of "duchies."

The party organizations are not strong enough to raise central campaign funds that can be allocated strategically, nor to lend important organizational assistance to candidates. This vacuum occasioned the formation of "unofficial" volunteer organizations in both parties—the California Republican Assembly and the California Democratic Council—which with varying degrees of success assumed the functions of candidate-screening and policy-formulating. But both organizations fell so far short of being strong mass-membership organizations that office-holders weren't inclined to pay them much heed, and candidates often didn't even seek their endorsement.

The California Democratic party now has an ostensible edge of some 1,370,000 registered adherents over the Republicans— 4,720,000 to 3,350,000. But a study of election results from 1958 on indicates that this margin is illusory.

Each party actually has a hard-core of around 2.5 million dependable voters. In addition, there are some one million voters who are registered as Democrats, and who sometimes vote Democratic—but just as often vote Republican, sometimes in the same election.

It was this critical swing vote, polarized toward the Democrats, that gave Brown his 1958 landslide; that in 1962 re-elected Senator Thomas Kuchel at the same time it was rejecting his fellow-Republican, Richard Nixon, for governor; that in 1964, while backing President Johnson to a man, simultaneously rejected Democrat Pierre Salinger for senator in favor of George Murphy; and that in 1966 gave Mr. Reagan his margin of nearly a million votes.

The critical nature of this swing vote has meant that, even as the radicals cavort on the fringes, the weight of the California electorate is centrist; a candidate who wants to win had best represent himself as a middle-road "moderate" in the context of the moment, who will not aggravate the chronic unsteadiness of the ship of state. It is probably this esteem for "moderation" that has given California government—as opposed to politics—its long-term stability.

Paradoxically, in an arena where party cohesion is so difficult to achieve, the penalty for disunity is inordinately high. The foremost axiom of California politics is that the party with a stiff primary fight is likely to lose the general election. Primary battles leave even the winner disheveled; the ammunition used against him within his own party is exploited afterward by the opposing party. California's temperamental electorate habitually turns its back on such candidates to support the party that has maintained a façade of unity. The indications in 1966 were that the Republicans would split over Reagan's "Goldwaterism" while the Democrats remained united. Just the opposite happened. Mr. Reagan submerged his right-wing past so effectively as to keep the Republicans together, while Los Angeles' Mayor Samuel Yorty, a party maverick, precipitated a Democratic split that was ruinous to Governor Brown.

This is California pragmatism.

As heretical a departure as it is from approved American political patterns, it has worked. It has maintained a remarkable degree of governmental efficiency and honesty during the hectic decades of California's rocketing growth into the nation's most populous state.

It has provided a climate for undertakings of unparalleled grandeur—the irrigation of the Central Valley to produce the nation's most abundant agricultural area; an unrivaled network of toll-less freeways and highways; the current two-billion-dollar, 500-mile-long water distribution project.

There are long-standing theories that the absence of "party responsibility" gives undue influence to lobbyists; and that the deficiencies in party organization have turned office-filling over to professional image-makers. But it has yet to be proved that these influences are any stronger than in other states.

Perhaps the severest criticism that can be made of the California pragmatic mode is its reckless squandering of manpower. Because office-holders have no opportunity, beyond abstract Warrenesque popularity, of cementing any following, the day a man goes out of office he represents one vote. California voters habitually turn their backs on defeated candidates. The list of living political has-beens is almost endless. Victories of Richard Nixon ended creditable careers of Representatives Jerry Voorhis and Helen Gahagan Douglas; in turn, Nixon's own defeat for governor in 1962 forced him to abandon his native state as a political base.

Yet altogether, California pragmatism, with all its oft-cited shortcomings, has yielded the "better life" sought by the pioneers, in such a degree that the trek toward it continues unabated.

California's choice of an actor to be governor reflected primarily its free-form nominating processes; and secondly, the perennial preference for what is conceived at the moment to be "moderation." But there may be national implications to the event. Some people see in this seemingly haphazard choice of a chief executive a symptom of the declining importance of state governments, which many observers have long lamented as abdicating their functions to direct federal-local relationships.

To some extent, certainly, the choice of a man admittedly inexperienced in politics and government suggests a realistic recognition by the electorate that government today actually is conducted by massive bureaucratic organisms of hired professionals— some 150,000 in the case of California; and a belief that leadership of such an organism is an inspirational rather than technological function. The existence of this feeling that specialized competence is irrelevant is further attested by the fact that Reagan was being talked about, far beyond the bounds of California, as presidential

timber long before anyone had a chance to see how he would perform as governor.

Where are California politics going?

There are obviously two possibilities: more of the same, or evolution toward a more stable, conventional two-party system.
At present, indications of the latter are scant.

There are leaders in both parties who are weary of the chronic
instability and wastefulness of pragmatism. They talk hopefully
of reviving partisan city and county politics as a step toward
statewide "party responsibility."

But at the same time there are those just as eager to further
weaken party lines by reviving cross-filing in modified form; all
candidates would be on a single primary ballot, and the highest-
scoring entries from the respective parties would be the run-off
contestants in the general election.

The electorate as a whole, insofar as it lends itself to any consideration as a whole, seems content with things as they are.

It can even be argued that the California approach to politics,
as in so many other fields, has simply anticipated national trends.

There is an obvious parallel between the submergence of partisan ideological lines in California, and the national movement
toward a "consensus" on broad questions, such as foreign policy,
that once formed the basis of party division. In the nation, as in
California, rival alignments have tended more and more toward a
generalized "go faster–go slower" argument than toward "issues,"
such as, for example, whether there should or should not be
publicly assisted housing.

The California pattern of a nominal Democratic electoral
majority that recurrently votes Republican, thanks to a large
"independent middle," actually mirrors the national situation.

Professor Bryce's observation that "The politics of California is
unique" endures, spectacularly unimpugned. But, on the basis of
the sheer arithmetic of human reproduction, the day is inexorably

approaching when most Californians will be natives of the state, and the giddy leavening growing out of individualistic immigration will dwindle away.

Then the question will be whether, with a relatively stable citizenry, California's poltics mature into a less pragmatic format— or whether California's atypicality of today becomes the typicality of tomorrow.

Art Seidenbaum

THE BLOODIEST BALLOT
IN THE UNITED STATES

In most populous California, voting is an enervating ordeal as well as a privilege. Possibly it was an accidental coincidence, but a majority of settlers would agree that what happened to one Albert Nickleby on election day, inside the privacy of a polling place at La Mirada, was symbolic of the strain in the democratic method.

Mr. Nickleby busted a blood vessel.

An undramatized account of this historic event is contained in an insurance claim, filed with the Los Angeles County Registrar by the woman in whose house it happened in November, 1966: "While Albert M. Nickleby, the last voter of the day, stood in the voting booth, a blood vessel in the lower portion of his neck ruptured and the loss of a great deal of blood resulted. The carpeting on which he stood became blood-soaked and subsequently

185

required the services of a professional rug cleaning service to remove the stain."

In one physical sense, voting in Los Angeles County can be a pleasure; more than 13,000 polling places, most of them in private homes, are within walking distance of the citizens. Good neighbors exchange pleasantries of the day coming and going. Good volunteers are congenial about passing out and collecting ballots.

In other ways, the procedure is punishing, primitive. A registered voter enters a booth smaller than one for public telephoning. On a belly-high slat of wood with no more surface than a rowboat seat, the citizen must mark a ballot that is sixteen and one-half inches wide and almost two feet long. If he is a meticulous voter, then he has likely brought his marked sample ballot, same size, with him; that means two pieces of paper which are larger than his table.

Equipment is also too small; the approved tool for exercising free choice is a rubber marker roughly one-third the size of a pencil. The marker, gummy from a previous voter's experience, is applied to ink pad and then to ballot.

The ritual is awkward and usually leaves apolitical smears on hands or clothing. Most Californians, in the most technologically-oriented state of this Union, vote without machines. Too expensive, say budget-broken officials. Too conducive to straight-ticket voting, claim many party mavericks. Although Los Angeles County has a large committee looking into the matter, they may look for years; no one seriously expects machines to replace gummy markers in the near future.

But it is the substance of voting, not the surroundings, that makes a citizen's life so difficult. A voter in the city of Los Angeles in 1966 had no fewer than forty-eight choices to make:

nine statewide offices, from governor down;

one congressional candidate to pick;

fourteen judges to approve or disapprove;

seventeen state measures, fifteen of them constitutional amendments, to mark yea or nay;
four county issues to decide;
two school tax questions to consider;
and one city charter amendment to resolve.

This was by no means an exceptional year. Attorney Paul
Ziffren, who once helped found the California Democratic Council
(to organize and mobilize liberal grass rooters), figures some
twenty measures are usually offered, not counting candidates or
judges, for voter decision.

The ballot length is preposterous, says editor Harry Ashmore,
now in residence at Santa Barbara's Center for the Study of
Democratic Institutions.

"People get bored by the time they get to the end," snorts
comedian Mort Sahl, not knowing that Nickleby had an opposite
sort of trouble.

By law, a Californian may spend ten minutes, no more, in the
privacy of his crude booth. The only way a sane man can elect
so many ambitious candidates and decide so many complicated
amendments in that time is by prior study.

The state does try to help him. Several days before any election, each registered voter receives a bulky packet from his county;
the packet tells him where to go on election day and provides him
with reading materials.

A Los Angeles packet this year held seven separate brochures
or papers:
one 38-page book full of micro-type contained pro-con dis-
cussions of the constitutional amendments;
a 4-page pamphlet considered the county measures;
a 32-page book of more mini-print was lavished on the proposed
city charter change.

A dutiful citizen spends his weekends prior to election hoping
to grasp, much less master, the legal wherefores and convoluted

advocacies in his ballot kit. There is no official count of busted blood vessels in home dens or reading chairs. And, naturally, all this matter comes to Californians in addition to the paper storm of gratuitous mailers, flyers, brochures, and biographies sent out by the interested parties of a two-party system.

How could such a thing happen to a nice state like this?

Most authorities blame the very constitution California is so constantly amending. UCLA political scientist Winston Crouch, co-author of *California Government and Politics,* says the ballot grows predictably out of the detailed and lengthy constitution drawn in 1879. It is the third longest document of its kind in the world and has already been bloated by more than three hundred amendments.

The provision for citizens' initiative, often cited by non-authorities as the chief villain, is not the reason for a ballooned ballot, but the initiative has been the cause of some of the wildest confusions and misguided conclusions in several election years.

Physician John R. Haynes of Los Angeles, a reformer with the finest intentions, was the force behind California's initiative and referendum (he also invented the recall method). Haynes did not trust legislators; he did trust the will of the people. When Progressive Hiram Johnson was elected governor in 1910, he brought the initiative with him in his platform. If 8 per cent of the electorate petition for a statute or for constitutional amendment, then such measure is placed on the ballot for voter resolution.

While it was born of idealism, the initiative has caused some historic mischief. In 1948, while the professionals were worrying more about candidates than initiatives, a bemused electorate passed a statute that transferred control of social welfare money to a man who had organized the old people for his own advantage. To undo the damage, a new constitutional amendment—the anti-measure—had to be passed two years later.

But 1964 was probably the all-time initiative absurdity, when California voters approved two separate initiatives which were later declared unconstitutional.

One was the famous Proposition Fourteen which repealed the Rumford Housing Act. Out of backlash, out of free enterprising, out of confusion, the voters chose to give property owners ultimate discriminatory powers in the sale or rental of housing.

The second was Proposition Seventeen to ban Pay-TV, sponsored and propagandized by theater owners who were afraid of counting empty houses if people could sit home with more sports and theatrical events. Out of ignorance the voters chose to keep pay television from brightening their doors.

While fear and honest conservatism might have explained Proposition Fourteen's success, there was no mollifying excuse for Proposition Seventeen's triumph over television. The people were fooled by a campaign that implied loss of free TV (certainly now one of the basic American freedoms) if Pay-TV were to be allowed in the home. Proponents' advertising was misleading and effective, despite no important newspaper, clergy, or political support.

"Use of the initiative," says Ashmore, "is deplorable. For a fee, you can buy a petition and get nearly anything put on the ballot. There are regular businesses for assuring signatures. A number of PR firms in California make a profession of collecting enough names to fill a petition; the going rate is now twenty-five cents per signature."

Whatever its noble origins, the initiative has lately become the most questionable single entry on an interminable ballot; instead of being responsive to the grass roots, it may now be a device for special interests, interests wealthy enough first to buy their way into an election and then to seduce the voters with come-on advertising.

In 1966, sixteen statewide measures were unfurled on the ballot by the California Legislature, fifteen of them constitutional amendments. Ashmore, Ziffren, and other students of the muddled system call this "buck-passing"; the politicians, instead of passing statutes, turn their problems over to the public. "You are asking the voter to legislate," grumbles Ziffren.

Not quite, argues Congressman Tom Rees, who used to be a state senator. Every measure on the ballot originating in Sacramento has to be approved for public vote by two-thirds of the legislature. "If you cut the constitution," claims Rees, "you will cut the ballot size."

Relief is coming. Proposition One-A in the last election was a first step in that direction. It was sponsored by the legislature, supported by both candidates for governor, and grew out of a 1962 statewide vote to lop off some of California's paper mountains. A Constitution Revision Commission of sixty-nine responsible citizens labored without pay for three years to bring One-A before the people.

Covering roughly one-third of the existing document, Proposition One-A slices 22,000 cumbersome, often gobbledygooking words into 6,000 reasonably understandable words. In the 38-page election primer from the seven-piece packet, One-A advocate Phil S. Gibson, former State Supreme Court Justice, said of California's constitution: "It is not only much too long, but it is almost everything a Constitution ought not to be."

"In short," argued a panel of official supporters, "it is a mess."

Some flavor of what a wordage mess may be about—including gracelessness—seeps out of the packet's printed argument against One-A submitted by California Assemblyman Leo J. Ryan: "As the only person who cast a negative vote in the Assembly on the Constitutional Revision program, under California law I am designated to submit the negative argument on Proposition One-A. At the time the vote was taken in the Assembly, I was not opposed to this proposition in its entirety; rather. I found fault with a few of its provisions . . ."

The punctuation around "rather," one has to believe, is an error by the state proofreader and not Mr. Ryan's diction. But when a whole hurry-up book has to be published in order to tell the voter what an election is about, such non-partisan accidents happen.

Proposition One-A passed.

Proposition Sixteen, the one fireworking initiative measure of 1966, did not. And its defeat, while unpredicted and unexpected, may be the most affirming gesture by California voters since Haynes' days.

This was the so-called CLEAN initiative, against obscenity. On the ballot, the words were: "Declares state policy is to prohibit obscene matter and conduct. Redefines 'obscene' and 'knowingly'; provides rules and procedures for prosecuting violations; jury unless waived determines amount of fine. Makes conspiracy to violate obscenity laws a felony. Authorizes seizure of obscene matter with procedure for summary determination of character. Requires vigorous enforcement and authorizes civil action to compel prosecutor to perform his duties."

To be "for" obscenity is a lonely position. After support for God and mother and flag, to oppose smut is part of the heritage. Here was a case of asking the electorate to mark a simple "x" against obscenity.

The proponents of Proposition Sixteen enjoyed an abundance of money along with their morality. Advertisements in behalf of CLEAN appeared all over the state; a handsome color supplement was inserted in major newspapers, advocating Sixteen and waggling that California is responsible for 60 per cent of the lewd matter manufactured in the United States. (To be first in population is progress; first in pornography is scandalous.)

The opponents of Sixteen were neither organized nor funded. A few weeks before the election, a private poll indicated that CLEAN would sweep (are puns obscene?) by a walloping two-to-one voter preference.

Yet in those few weeks, several things happened, all of them overdue bouquets for democracy. Prominent clergymen announced their disapproval of Sixteen. So did the California Library Association. So did several law enforcement officers. And so did many powerful newspapers. While there was no amalgamation of negative voices and no real anti-CLEAN campaign launched, opposition was coming from respectable sources.

The Board of Directors of the Northern California Council of Churches said the proposition was so broad that, if adopted, Sixteen might even prohibit the Bible or Shakespeare.

The district attorney of Los Angeles County, along with other experts, announced that Sixteen, if passed, was likely to be declared unconstitutional. That would be three in a row for the initiative and it might leave the state with no obscenity law of any kind.

One of the keys to CLEAN, not explained on the ballot, was that the measure would eliminate from the penal code a phrase that defines obscenity as matter "utterly without redeeming social importance." But how could scholars expect common men to understand that anti-obscenity, when applied crudely, might be more dangerous than obvious pornography?

The voter, experts mourned in advance, is not sufficiently sophisticated to make such distinctions.

Governor Ronald Reagan, while never announcing in favor of Sixteen, also refused to repudiate the measure, claiming that he approved the spirit if not the specifics of the initiative.

Robert Finch, Reagan's running mate, did announce against Sixteen: "Everyone said I was crazy to come out against Sixteen, but I hung my hat on it." Not only did the measure lose, Finch ran ahead of his entire ticket, cadging more votes than any Republican in California history.

The result was astonishing, yet it happened. The defeat of CLEAN was a clear vindication of the voter. He did read. He did study. He did learn some lessons from the debacle of 1964. Now super-sophisticates are saying that the analogy between Sixteen of '66 and Seventeen of '64 is not valid because voting against a loudly promoted CLEAN initiative did not cost the voter anything. In 1964, the voter was afraid that Pay-TV would cost him free depilatory commercials.

But there is no denying that the voter operated selectively in 1966, somehow managing to wade through the shrieking advertisements and cooing blandishments to make up his own mind before coping with the gummy marker.

The skeptical Mr. Sahl has worried that ballots are always worded in "quadruple negatives" so that "you don't know what you're voting on anyway." In the past this has been true; many people who voted for Proposition Fourteen in 1964 thought they were advancing the cause of integration rather than retarding it.

And there was one curious result in 1966. A statewide bond issue to provide college construction funding was passed. Two Los Angeles County measures to raise tax funding for public schools failed. College won; junior college and grammar school lost. Obviously, citizens will authorize bonds more readily than taxes.

In approving constitutional revision, the voters have at last begun to make their own deciding lives easier. Winston Crouch would remind the citizens that the initiative process is not bad in itself; the state budget system, the voter registration law, and the State Civil Service Commission—all healthy examples of good law-giving—were the products of the initiative. "If you only look at a couple of years," says Crouch, "you are likely to have a skewed picture of measures petitioned by the people."

Right now, the state courts have been asked to nullify three propositions that passed in November, including the constitution-shrinking One-A. A group called the California State Federation of Civic Improvement Clubs Inc. (pity the printer if that title has to be on a ballot) are challenging the system on the familiar grounds that only vested interests can afford to put a measure on the ballot.

In 1911, says the federation, only 50,000 signatures were needed to qualify under the 8 per cent rule. Today, an initiative petition has to have 500,000 names. The federation would have the propositions declared null on grounds that they reflect "the intent of public officers to diminish the constitutional rights of the people."

Such efforts—apparently more anti-legislature than anti-initiative—are likely to fail but they do point up the continuing confusions of being a Californian. And while a Superior Court considers this suit, the United States Supreme Court is examining the famous Proposition Fourteen of 1964. The California Supreme Court declared the measure unconstitutional because it made government an accessory to discrimination. The sponsors of the measure, including the California Realtors Association, have appealed that decision to the highest court.

Mr. Nickleby and his millions of fellow sufferers may find the marking clearer in 1968. The pressures for shorter ballots, shapelier constitution, better ballot language are bi-partisan and growing louder all the time. Machines may be a millenium off for mammoth Los Angeles, but fresh respect for the solitary man in the makeshift booth is more than a trend.

And the attempts to make the government more responsive to the governed may be more historically important than California's willingness to cast actors in unfamiliar roles.

15

Scott Thurber

CONSERVATION
COMES OF AGE

"To become a conservationist in California," a leader in the field remarked recently with blunt accuracy, "all you have to do is look around you." Since the mid-1940s California has been disfiguring itself to accommodate the incoming hordes. Today the Californian can still see much of the rare natural beauty that attracted him to the state in the first place, but he also sees the instruments of its destruction hard at work. Chain saws are felling the forests, bulldozers are decapitating hilltops and filling valleys in the path of broad concrete freeways, and the orchards and fields are giving way to endless rows of die-stamped tract houses, the slums of the future. Smog infests the air, and the streams and roadsides are polluted with the rubbish of a no-deposit, no-return civilization.

The conservationist has traditionally been something of an eccentric—shouting alarms, putting out brush fires. But today there is a difference: he is being heard—and attended. His ranks are swelling; he has, indeed, become respected. More important, he has become effective, and nowhere is this change more apparent than in California, a clearly threatened last frontier of outstanding natural environment.

"We Americans have never been at peace with our environment," the noted architect and conservationist, Nathaniel Owings, remarked recently. "We've always believed in an endless wilderness. If we cut one forest and built a town, there was always another forest just over the hill. In planning we've never treated our environment as an equal."

The fact that our wilderness is not endless, that in fact we are coming to the end of it, has in recent years become a matter of mounting concern to a steadily increasing number of Californians. The growth of California's conservation movement has been dramatically evident since about 1947, when a restless postwar population began pushing into the state. Today—with an estimated 1,500 newcomers arriving in the state daily—it is at its peak thus far in numbers, diversity and accomplishments.

Ad hoc organizations are formed in response to specific situations. One of these fought to block an Atomic Energy Commission power line projected to run through the scenic San Francisco Peninsula community of Woodside, and had to settle for a "compromise" that was largely a loss; another kept Pacific Gas and Electric Company from building a nuclear power plant on Bodega Head on the rugged northern coast. At the same time, permanent, single-purpose organizations have proliferated. Some of them are statewide, like the California Roadside Council; some are regional, like the Committee for Green Foothills or the League to Save Lake Tahoe, and some are small, local, and terribly specialized. There are also the big, long-established conservation organizations —the Save-the-Redwoods League and the Sierra Club—both founded and based in California, but both with nationwide memberships and influence.

The individual and sometimes collective energy of all these organizations—big, small, permanent, and one shot—of late has yielded some heartening results. A few examples:

¶ California voters in 1964 approved a bond issue of $150 million for park purchase and development; $85 million was earmarked—and is now being spent—to buy and preserve new parklands, something like 265,000 acres in all.

¶ Conservationists have beaten back an attempt by the highway engineers to bulldoze a freeway through a choice part of northern California's virgin redwood forest.

¶ The state is setting out to create the first portions of what ultimately would be a 4,000-mile system of parkways—low-speed, pleasure-driving roadways through elongated parks. The antithesis of freeways.

¶ An official state commission has been created to stop the filling of San Francisco Bay and to study all aspects of its permanent preservation.

¶ The voters have created a special sort of "green-belt" zoning that will protect a farmland owner from spiraling tax assessments if he agrees to keep the land open and undeveloped for a specified period of years.

¶ Pacific Gas and Electric, which learned some sobering truths about conservation and public opinion in the Bodega Head battle, has started seeking the advice of conservationists before planning new plants.

And there has been still another development which might be said to reflect the growing political maturity of the state's conservation groups: they have banded together to hammer out a wide-ranging legislative program, and hired a lobbyist to work for its enactment in Sacramento.

Nothing better illustrates the growth, scope, and vigor of the California conservation movement than the Sierra Club, probably the largest and most effective conservation force in the country, and certainly the best known. The Sierra Club is something of an elder statesman of conservation. It was founded some seventy-five years ago by the naturalist John Muir. From the outset it was an organization to preserve outstanding samples of our environment. One of Muir's (and the club's) signal achievements was the preservation of California's magnificent Yosemite Valley. Yet in Muir's time and into ours the club has been best known for its expeditions which took members—hikers, campers, back packers, and the like—into Muir's beloved Sierra and other wilderness regions. In 1947, the club had a large number of hikers, a small staff, about 4,000 members, and an annual budget of about $100,000.

The Sierra Club still has a lot of hikers—including those who trek into the Sierra each year to haul out the incredible array of refuse left behind by despoiling vacationists. But the club's principal concern, its major activity as an organization, has become the conservation of natural beauty. Currently, it has 47,000 members, and an annual budget of almost $2 million. Those figures are on the scale of a respectably large corporation, and the club is in corporation-type trouble with Washington.

The person most responsible for what the Sierra Club is today— for the stands it takes, its public image, the attention it gets and, indeed, its current fight with the Internal Revenue Service—is David Brower, the organization's $18,000-a-year executive director. An expert mountaineer and a veteran of the Army's 10th Mountain Division, Brower is immensely well informed and possessed of an unswerving dedication to the causes in which he believes. He is also something of a rarity: a zealot with a sense of humor. Even his enemies—and these currently must include many dam builders and tree cutters in government as well as industry—regard him with a respect tinged with awe.

Brower, of course, doesn't run the club by himself. He recommends policies with a knowledgeable persuasiveness, but the policies are set by a board of directors that has impressive credentials of its own. It currently includes the celebrated naturalist-photographer Ansel Adams; Dr. William Siri, a University of California biophysicist and expert mountaineer who was deputy chief of the United States team which scaled Mount Everest in 1963; Dr. Edgar Wayburn, prominent internist, Medical Society activist, political conservative, and conservation liberal who for years has been in the vanguard of the club's major battles.

The club went into the book-publishing field a few years ago, and its program has been rewarding. The volumes in the "Exhibit Format Series" are beautifully designed and printed, combining breath-taking photography with evocative texts. They are expensive ($17.50; $25) and the profit from their sale has become a major source of finances for the club's conservation program. Above all, the books tell the story of conservation—and tell it well. The moods range from the quiet persuasiveness of *This Is The American Earth* to the more urgent tone of *The Last Redwoods* and *Time and the River Flowing: Grand Canyon,* which show what's at stake in the club's two biggest current battles.

Dave Brower's first major triumph for the Sierra Club was the successful campaign to save Dinosaur National Monument from inundation behind a Bureau of Reclamation power dam in Echo Park. That battle bore a striking similarity to the club's present campaign to save the Grand Canyon—a campaign which is still far from won.

Two dams are proposed—one upstream from Grand Canyon National Park and one downstream from the National Monument, but both within the canyon proper. Again, power is involved— and, of course, the Bureau of Reclamation. The dams would be built as part of the Central Arizona Project—a plan that is politically sensitive because it involves a long-sought water-sharing agreement among the Colorado River Basin states. The Sierra Club contends that the proposed dams—at Marble Gorge and Bridge Canyon—would forever destroy the Colorado as "a living river"—and that they are wholly unnecessary because they wouldn't conserve a drop of water. They would, instead, simply be "cash registers"—producing salable hydroelectric power.

The dams are a threat to more than the ancient majesty of the Grand Canyon. As Brower puts it: "What is at stake is the entire conservation movement, and a brilliant national park system. If Grand Canyon can be destroyed, then no parks, wilderness or wild rivers can be considered safe."

The club said all that, and more, in the now historic full-page advertisements it published in The Washington *Post* and *The New York Times* on June 8, 1966. Less than twenty-four hours after their appearance, the club was informed that the Internal Revenue Service had started an investigation to determine whether it should lose its tax-deductible status because it was spending a "substantial part" of its income on "influencing legislation." Nearly six months later—after a period of uncertainty which cost the club an estimated $125,000 in withheld contributions—the IRS decreed, in a tentative ruling, that the club is no longer eligible to receive "deductible charitable contributions." The key words "substantial" and "influence" are nowhere defined.

The club spent $10,000 on the ads that provoked IRS' Instant Wrath (seldom in history has a federal bureaucracy reacted with such cobralike speed). Many other tax-deductible organizations, which lobby blatantly and on a much grander scale, have been left untouched by the IRS. The Central Arizona Project Association, for instance, spent $74,065.02 in 1965 to advocate the dams the club opposes. The association's tax-deductible status remains in force.

Permanent loss of its tax-deductible status would hurt but not cripple the club's conservation program. It would impede the flow of big cash gifts and bequests—it's fashionable to mention conservation groups in your will these days—but the club has other resources: due, fees for outings, book sales, to keep it going. Incidentally, the effect of the IRS battle hasn't been all bad: when the investigation was first announced, the club had 38,000 members; today it has more than 47,000.

The Sierra Club is skirmishing on many fronts. It is concerned for the future of the Florida Everglades, Storm King Mountain on the Hudson, and the forests of the Oregon Cascades. In its home state, it vigorously pursues causes, large and small. Its San Francisco Bay chapter is in the forefront of a move to forestall a major commercial development in the middle of the Bolinas Lagoon, a significant wildlife sanctuary on the Marin County coastline north of San Francisco. On a larger scale, the club is working to create a Redwood National Park on Redwood Creek in Humboldt County—"the last opportunity for a *real* Redwood National Park." (The Administration, in the Eighty-Ninth Congress, backed a hastily prepared proposal for a smaller park on Mill Creek in Del Norte County—an area the club contends has been heavily logged over. Almost all major conservation groups backed the club's proposal at hearings held in 1966.)

In 1966, the club's directors took an unprecedented stand: they endorsed the site of a proposed PG&E nuclear power plant on the San Luis Obispo County coastline. This provoked an internal fight which still continues. The recommended site at Diablo Canyon was backed by the directors—however reluctantly and conditionally—as preferable to the utility's first choice of Nipomo Dunes in the same county, a spectacular and unspoiled area the club has long fought to preserve as a state park. The majority view of the board of directors is that it was either Diablo Canyon or Nipomo Dunes—and that the club can't simply oppose but must offer intelligent co-operation in matters like this. The dissidents argue that it wasn't an either-or situation, that the utility had other alternatives, and that Diablo Canyon is well worth saving on its own merits. Since the directors have refused to back down, their decision will now be subjected to a membership referendum, first of its kind in the club's history.

One of the admitted shortcomings of the California conservation movement in the past has been its disorganized concentration on, to a large degree, defensive warfare: reacting to provocation, rushing here and there in defense of something threatened—be it Bolinas Lagoon, San Francisco Bay, or a pristine redwood grove. A major and co-ordinated attempt at a systematic new approach to the preservation of the environment is now beginning in California, and some conservationists regard it as the most significant development in many years. The groups—large and small—have banded together into a special-purpose organization, the Planning and Conservation League, that also includes such related interests as the statewide organizations of architects, landscape architects, and designers. Its single purpose: effective legislation in the conservation field.

At a recent daylong seminar in Berkeley, the new league hammered out a co-ordinated program of proposed legislation, ranging from a law to ban smog-producing vehicles from the state's highways by 1980 to a law that would flatly forbid highway engineers from invading parklands without the unlikely advance consent of the State Park Commission. The Planning and Conservation League will press its legislative goals in Sacramento through the office of a full-time professional lobbyist.

Nothing exactly like this has ever been done before in California conservation, and many regard the effort as long overdue. "At last," a leader in the group reflected recently, "we are making the transition from little old lady in tennis shoes to effective political activist."

Robert Kirsch

THE CULTURAL SCENE

Is it a cultural boom, explosion, renaissance, this thing in California? A little of each, yet none of the terms describes it adequately. The scene is booming—two new theaters in the Los Angeles Music Center complex are ready to open; San Francisco's refurbished Palace of Fine Arts is nearing completion; a city of 30,000 like Santa Maria supports an astonishing variety of concerts, theater, art exhibits; the colleges and universities provide creative writing programs, ambitious fine arts programs, lectures, extension instruction.

But there are disturbing omens of bust, as well. Only a desperate last minute three-day fund drive raised the money to settle a labor dispute with the musicians of the Los Angeles Philharmonic. This saved the 1966–67 season but was far from a permanent solution. San Francisco trounced a bond issue for modernization of its opera house and museum; a theater-in-the-round couldn't make it in the bustling culture-hungry San Fernando Valley. And perhaps most threatening, the dynamic system of public higher education, which is the single most important source of the culture boom, is threatened with severe budget cutbacks.

Sometimes things explode with a bang, other times end with a whimper. A few galleries closed in 1967; others reported a 10–20 per cent loss of sales. That staple trait of California culture, dedicated amateurism, is still much in evidence. The trend is toward expression, awareness, creativity; sometimes the whole state seems one arts and crafts therapy session. But there is fall-out. Questions of quality are being raised. And questions of motivation. Finance is a problem of sufficient magnitude that one newspaper headlined a symposium on the arts in California, "The Crisis in Culture." The crisis? Money. The solution, more government support, a broader base of private and corporate contributions. The Los Angeles Philharmonic receives contributions from only seven thousand of the estimated seven million people living in the Los Angeles metropolitan area.

Local government support is not without its strings. The County Board of Supervisors, whose members are political geiger counters, has used its financial power to threaten the Art Museum over its Edward Kienholz exhibit, has warned the new Center Theater Group to cleanse its selection of plays.

Is it a renaissance? Hardly. Stretch the word, allow for the congenital California hyperbole, and maybe the word has some relevance. California has a past in the arts, in music, literature, architecture, painting. But the present surge is hardly a rebirth, certainly not a rediscovery of heritage. If anything, the trend is ignorance of the past. California is mainly present-oriented, shallow-rooted, amnesic.

Something is going on. The cultural scene today is a complex viral happening, somewhere between chemistry and life, between health and illness, expressed in action, disparate aches and fevers, dizziness and euphoria, hallucinations and moments of reality.

Symptoms are contradictory; diagnosis is virtually impossible. By the time you have isolated one virus, another has started its life cycle. And everything overlaps. High culture co-exists with *kitsch;* tradition with innovation; excellence with mediocrity; the authentic with the phoney; freedom of expression with a deep impulse to censor and suppress. The mixture is unlikely as California itself, vast, sprawling, heterogeneous, surprising.

This sense of activity which stirred the English novelist T. H. White to compare California, particularly Southern California, to Elizabethan London, does exist. Something of the hungers, aspirations, mobility, confidence of the region, gives relevance to the notion. It seems to recapitulate, with acceleration and intensity, the conditions of other cultural blossomings in New York, Boston, Chicago.

Whatever else it may be, California is a microcosm of America in the age of affluence, leisure, and education. Thoreau wrote, "In dreams, we see ourselves naked and acting out our real characters, even more closely than we see others awake." California is America's dream whether the rest of the country is ready to admit it or not. Enough people vote by airline ticket, bus ride, or Route 66 in their tens of thousands every month, to make the claim believable. And of those who do not come to California, the place inhabits a realm of the imagination. All are caught up in the surreality of it, contribute their private visions or nightmares. Someone has said that California is the place where the ideal self comes closest to realization. If this is so, we are given an extraordinary profile of America's aspirations and fears. That is why the cultural scene in California, at any level, is significant to the country at large. They must see themselves, caricatured, perhaps, but reflected nevertheless. It accounts for the conflicted responses toward California. Thoreau touched it: "But an unwavering and commanding virtue would compel even its most fantastic and faintest dreams to respect its ever-wakeful authority; as we are accustomed to say carelessly, we should never have dreamed of such a thing."

This sense of California as projection has always been viable. In today's world, seamed together by jets, by instantaneous mass communication, California's general ties have merged into a chaotic day-to-day detail. Whatever occurs, no matter how trivial, how ludicrous, how ephemeral, is on everybody's television screen the same night, in their newspapers the next morning. Nothing has a chance to crystallize, so everything accelerates like a speeded-up movie film. Before the Sunset Strip calmed down after its hippy ferment, anthropologists were analyzing it in *The New York Review of Books*. A graduate student at Stanford hastened to record his observations of California conversational style in *Harper's* as he returned East after a three-year stay. Richard Todd writes:

> For some, to be sure, openness in speech is more than an occasional matter, even more than a habit: it is a code. The code not only prohibits indirection, but frowns on the use of the conventional language of social deceit. A successful California dinner party may suddenly swerve into failure with the conventional closing lines: "It was nice to see you." Suddenly everyone is on edge, a social blunder has occurred: the offender was speaking artificially, not of the self.

Whether Todd is right or wrong in his magisterial pronouncement is of less consequence than that he found the material for it. Traveling in other circles he might have uncovered supporting anecdotes for precisely the opposite point of view. If California did not exist, America would have had to invent it; it provides too much copy to be dispensable. And America did invent it, provided the cost, collaborates on the script. This is the crux of the present California; it interacts closely and immediately with the rest of the country. Distance and remoteness have disappeared. In cultural terms, both high and general, there is an increasing fusion. Theater groups such as Ellis Rabb's APA divide their time among New York, Los Angeles, Ann Arbor; William Ball and his ACT Repertory will be shared between New York and Chicago. Martin Bernheimer, music critic for the Los Angeles *Times,* suggests that Los Angeles "become an operatic partner with another city." San Francisco, San Diego, Boston, Dallas are possibilities. Actors Studio West is an offshoot of the New York group.

The liaison is far from complete. California is too vast for that. Most people think of Los Angeles and San Francisco. But California is composed of smaller cities, jealous of their identity and prerogatives: Santa Barbara, Bakersfield, Stockton, San Diego, Fresno. It has a hinterland of small towns and rural areas as well. This complicates any effort to capture the total scene. California is huge, roiling, vivid, journalistic, serious, arid, creative, silly, profound, radical, moderate, intelligent, and stupid.

Lately, with rare exceptions it has been having a favorable press. The new thing is to praise California. This too will pass, but it was intoxicating for a while, especially with its former concerns about what the rest of the country thought of it. California doesn't give a damn. Art Seidenbaum, a discerning commentator on the California scene, suggests that there are three phases in California's development. He calls them the *Kook Phase,* the *Window on Tomorrow* or *Test of the Future,* and the *Open Skull Phase.* All three co-exist, though the last is predominant. Letting the rest of the country see how we think is part of the self-critical era. Herbert Gold's piece on San Francisco writers in *The New York Times Book Review,* February, 1967, could not have been written five years ago when the booster cycle was still operative. San Francisco writing is mostly talk and it is acceptable to say so.

The race riots in Los Angeles and San Francisco had something to do with this new ventilation of soul-searching. For a state which had prided itself on being the Promised Land for minorities (without much hard evidence to support it), the illusion was shattered in Watts and Hunters Point. Boosterism is an extreme extension of pride, and pride is at its best with a certain humility. That appears to be developing in a self-criticism which is the healthiest sign on the cultural scene.

Seen from close up, the cultural scene in California is far from realized. It has had its successes and failures, built its edifices, has yet to fill them with works of excellence. There is a phenomenon in the California deserts which only experienced walkers know: distances are deceptive. In that clear air are not only mirages, but something even more illusory. Standing on the desert floor, the mountains may seem an hour's hike away when, in fact, they may be fifty long miles distant. The same sort of illusion captivates Californians, and outsiders, when they consider the cultural scene. They have the sense of being at the proximate edge of a fulfilled achievement. They are miles away.

For example, Assembly Bill One, introduced by Jesse M. Unrah, Speaker of the California Assembly, in 1963, signed into law by then Governor Edmund G. Brown, established a California Arts Commission, with a view, the enabling legislation went, "to establish the paramount position of this State in the nation and the world as a cultural center."

The rhetoric was pure California, with a touch of Hollywood in "paramount." Brown appointed Abbott Kaplan, then head of UCLA's phenomenally successful Extension Division, as chairman of an impressive commission. Novelist Martin Dibner was named executive director. The commission, on a meager budget of $100,000 or so, organized traveling exhibits, symposia, consulted with local arts councils, encouraged activities in theater, film, music, painting. Like every public body in California, it sponsored a survey, published in 1966 as "The Arts in California," beautifully printed and illustrated, concluded with an admirably accurate summary ("Interest and activity in the arts in California have grown impressively in recent years, but unevenly in quality and distribution.") and an ambitious program for encouragement of the arts.

Now, the fate of the commission is uncertain. California's contradictory personality would not be denied. With Governor Reagan's austerity budget, funds are likely to be cut drastically. In any case, Brown is gone. Unruh has turned from cultural concerns to another art form: re-designing the decimated Democratic party. Kaplan leaves for New York to head a new college there. Dibner is in Maine, finishing a novel. One thing is certain: "the paramount position of this State in the nation and the world as a cultural center" is far from established.

But the great cultural happening goes on. The patterns are not clear. Neil Morgan, columnist for the San Diego *Evening Tribune* and author of two discerning books on the westward tilt, calls it "a putty culture, not yet hardened into shape," borrowing from designer Charles Eames, long a critic of the "esthetic nightmare" of Southern California. Eames explains the cultural nihilism of the place as a result of "the absence of social and physical restraints" and because the people are "a less sensitive group than any other." The absence of restraint, of standards, of a sense of the past, Eames compares to a sculptor's work in plasteline. "One can do any imaginable variety of bad without half trying. The material puts up no resistance and whatever discipline there is, the artist must be strong enough to provide."

A few can, many don't. Yet, there are signs that the amorphous mass is hardening into some shape. Resistances are developing: California's critics are becoming less provincial, unwilling to accept a performance or a painting simply because it is by one of their own. Not too many years ago, a professor who had written a play to be presented in one of the local theaters, contributed a long essay to one of the Los Angeles papers, arguing that his work should be given special attention simply because it was a local product. Such provincialism might occur in one of the smaller towns, but it seems hardly possible now in Los Angeles, if it ever was in San Francisco.

Audiences are growing more discerning, less hospitable to the mediocre, although there is still a strong tendency toward the outer-directed, status-motivated attendance at cultural events. It is still possible to hear a Los Angeles audience give generous applause to a second-rate Broadway actor in a road show play just as he appears on the stage, and before he utters a word.

There is a resistance in the hard facts of the performing arts, in supporting orchestras and museums, financing theaters, building attendance, not to mention the constant contention in the dialectic of California, issues of free expression and censorship. The traditional citrus Bible belt of Southern California still has its adherents but an antithetical group of academics, professionals, and intellectuals has been able to parry most of their attacks. It is a good augury that the electorate which gave Reagan a landslide victory defeated convincingly the infamous CLEAN amendment which he and his monied backers supported.

Sometimes, the putty culture can produce something strikingly original such as Simon Rodia's great primitive creation, fashioned from the rubble of civilization, even, as some might say, as Los Angeles itself. Characteristically, the City Building Department tried to tear it down (inexplicably, it met all the stress tests) but the community mobilized effectively to save it.

An emerging sense of the past saved San Francisco's mouldering Palace of Fine Arts, a not unattractive mélange of Greek and Roman styles built fifty-two years ago to last the summer of the International Exposition of 1915. Now at a cost of seven million dollars, the Palace is being transmuted from plaster and wood into concrete and steel. The state put up two million dollars on condition that it be made into a State Park and leased back to the city for "cultural, recreational, educational, museum, artistic or musical exposition purposes."

What are they going to do with the giant structure, which stretches the length of three football fields? Well, here we have that strange California mentality at work. One group led by a justice of the State Supreme Court has suggested (and not entirely in a kidding way) the installation of indoor tennis courts. Others have urged bowling, skating, educational TV studios, a music conservatory, a little theater, a museum, or an exhibition hall for trade shows.

Another suggestion that it be used as an academy for the performing arts, run by the state college system, has been shelved because of the current financial difficulties in higher education. And the Palace of Fine Arts is far from through with its own money worries. It is going to take another million dollars just to provide adequate lighting, heating, and sprinkler systems against fire, not to mention furnishings and decoration. The Palace of Fine Arts League, in typical California style, is unmoved by these practical considerations. It is going ahead with a planned ten-day festival of the arts to raise $200,000 to assist in the completion of the structure.

The Palace is symbolic of the edifice complex which has seized California. But we are learning that what you put into buildings is what counts. And that support of the arts is a continuing obligation.

Yet, the lesson is not that well taken as we see down south in that center of finance and fine arts, Beverly Hills, one of the richest cities of the world (it sits on a pool of oil). The season of the new Beverly Hills Symphony Orchestra ended after two performances in the posh room of a local hotel. One was conducted by Igor Stravinsky, the other by Johnny Green. Again, the reason was lack of funds. The real reason: Beverly Hills just doesn't want to be bothered. The mayor announced he was shocked—"There is no reason why the community can't support an orchestra." When asked if the city government would help, he was even more shocked, explaining city funds were "too meager" for such a project. Considering that one of the current notions about the arts in California is that it is turning from its traditional amateur base to professionalism (the Beverly Hills orchestra lasted eighteen years as a do-it-yourself activity), it would seem the new look is still largely putty.

There is, then failure and success, false starts and dead ends.
Some of the great achievements such as the Tamarind Print Workshop project headed by June Wayne remain almost unpublicized,
though generously supported by foundation funds; some of the
highly publicized ventures such as the Los Angeles Art Museum
have been through rocky times. On the one hand, a community
mobilized to save bankrupt Pasadena Playhouse (in a script which
could have been written by Dion Boucicault); on the other, San
Francisco lets its Actors Workshop go to pieces. The Los Angeles
Public Library, one of the busiest and most starved financially, is
seeking voter approval for a bare-bones 57-million-dollar expansion program to serve the pituitary growth of the city. There
seems at this moment little chance that it will pass. Although,
again, no one who has been through the California experience will
bet against the possibility that it will pass overwhelmingly.

There is an appetite for culture and a deep sense that the
moment is at hand to accomplish it. Dr. Kaplan, the philosopher
of the culture boom in California, quotes the words of John
Adams (a favorite quotation out here now):

"I must study politics and war so that my sons may have the
liberty to study mathematics, philosophy and commerce so that
their children may have the right and privilege to study painting,
poetry and music."

It is, again in characteristic California ways, all going on at
once. The youthful subculture of California is vigorous, wild, re-
bellious, and basically healthy. Despite the impatience with the
Berkeley unrest, the hippies, the underground newspapers, all
of these are very much a part of the California cultural scene.
After all, it is this open intellectual and artistic environment which
encourages the kind of challenge which youth represents in this
child-centered state.

If high culture is supported by the well-to-do, there is a strong
infusion of younger, less affluent contributors as well. Theater has
captured the imagination of these people. Lew Wasserman, head

of Universal Studios, president of the Center Theater Group, is optimistic that the estimated annual deficit of the Mark Taper Forum (about $250,000) will be taken up by contributions from the younger executives in business. "Most of the management of the major companies are young men—and the theatre, more than dance or music, appeals to the young. If it is the sort of stimulating, abrasive, cerebral theatre, relevant to our times, we hope to do."

Gordon Davidson, artistic director of the Center Theater Group, who came with his company from UCLA's Extension Division, plans a major student program. Youth attendance at California theaters is estimated to be over 20 per cent of the total audience.

The best hope for a continuation of the cultural surge is the intensification of community identification which comes from the provision of amenities such as museums, concert halls, theaters. Much will depend on the situation of the institutions of higher learning which, in alliance with civic-minded benefactors, provide the stimulus and wherewithal. The Arts Commission study found that "communities with an institution of higher learning" experience a sharp increase in cultural activities. There is evidence that the business community is willing to back up its interest with contributions. In Santa Maria, it was the inquiries by firms planning to settle in that community about cultural activities which persuaded city government to support the efforts of private groups in that pursuit.

All of this provides an atmosphere of encouragement to artists. California offers a choice of solitude or contact, a relatively easy way of life, perhaps for some too easy. Artists too are migrating here and have been for many years.

A cultural scene, active, contradictory, filled with potential, sometimes realized. Perhaps in the end what will realize a cultural renaissance in California is the very element which makes it so amorphous at present, the people who come here. They provide both creator and consumer. And they are touchingly eloquent in their comments. A woman member of the Red Bluffs Art Association says: "Other than facilities and funds . . . our greatest need would seem to be to bring the outside world of art to our area . . . one must have exposure to good art to enjoy and appreciate it."

Or, the words of Margarette Brown Meggs, a member of the City Council of Grass Valley (population 4,876) in Nevada County, in a letter to the California Arts Commission:

> We are one of the poorest cities in the State in culture of any kind. Our children are deprived of the very knowledge that such órganizations as those devoted to cultural and artistic pursuits exist . . . You could very well take your entire budget and spend it here in Grass Valley. . . . Our neighbor four miles to the east, Nevada City, is more progressive. They have recently formed an arts group but it is theirs. However we share with them the Twin Cities Concert Association which brought three concerts to this area last year. Hoorah! Having heard *Salome* last week at the new Music Center in Los Angeles, I can only cry, HELP GRASS VALLEY.

Super-sincere and turned-on? Yes, but not the least impressive potential of the cultural scene here is in terms of people like Mrs. Meggs of Grass Valley. In the end, a cultural renaissance is produced by audiences, discovering the arts, as well as by the artists who serve their needs. Both exist here.

We have spoken of culture in California. Is there a California culture? San Francisco poet Kenneth Rexroth sees it as developing in conflict and blending, between old and new, between "get yours and get out" and the idea of putting something back. "The old Puritan ethic, shaped in conflict with an environment of storms and violent changes in weather, seems to be replaced, in widely varying degree, by the old *'vie Méditerranée'* of interpersonal laissez faire and *dolce far niente* of wide tolerance and easy manners."

Symbols of this are in San Francisco, "the only northern city in the United States untouched by the overland spread of the New

England Puritan tradition" and Los Angeles, where "more people have migrated . . . since the last war than took part in all the Great Migrations at the end of the Roman Empire." And all the points in between, a scattering of towns much like those in every part of the American hinterland.

He continues: ". . . What is certain is that although the old external frontier has largely passed away, a new internal frontier has opened out, into a new kind of life, and the possibility at least of profound changes in the quality of that life."

Rexroth sees it as nothing less than the expression of a cultural worldwide revolution, bringing new kinds of language and literature, new kinds of music and painting, "and, more fundamentally, a new attitude toward life."

Exuberant and prophetic, yet his words invoke some of the sense of the place, the spirit which informs the scene. Tomorrow, perhaps, or after, there will be a California culture. Meanwhile, even the outsiders sense it. Art Critic Barbara Rose can write: "Visiting the galleries along La Cienega, one begins to picture Europe as the Renaissance, New York as the Avant Garde and L. A. as the 'orgiastic future' that year by year becomes more actual and immediate, replete with an art already actual and immediate."

Or, T. H. White, who recorded in his journal on what was to be his final trip to California:

"I don't mind if the beauty is a bit cockeyed sometimes, like the Grauman Theatre or even the wildest excesses of de Mille. The point is that the money *is* being spent on culture of some sort, that it is an individual culture, and that even millionaires care about it."

Out here, we are impatient. It is part of the air we breathe. But sometimes, in some small way, we have a glimpse of what it will be like when the mountains are reached.

R. T. Appleyard

WESTWARD
THE ANTIPODES

My task is to examine the proposition that, inasmuch as the "pioneer spirit" still exists in America, it is more likely to be found in California migrants and their children than in established easterners. There is no reason, so the argument runs, why the westward frontier should be stopped by the Pacific or why the pioneer who has reached its shores should "sit himself down and 'weep for other worlds.' "[1] Seven thousand miles farther westward lies a country as geographically large as America, a country with enormous natural resources and inhabited by only eleven million English-speaking Caucasians who, next to North Americans, enjoy the highest per capita income in the world. A century

---

[1] See Ray Allen Billington, *America's Frontier Heritage,* Holt, Rinehart and Winston, New York, 1966, pp. 190–191. This is the comment by a British visitor to America in the 1820s who believed the pioneer "had always something better in his eye, further west . . . ."

ago, the pioneers looked across the Mississippi, packed their bags, and in covered wagons journeyed westward to make their fortune and to share in a fresh civilization. Today Americans still look westward, not from the shores of the Mississippi but from the shores of the Pacific, and many of them have packed their bags and, in Boeing 707's, journeyed westward to make their fortunes to share in the fresh Australian civilization.

"If students of American character," writes Billington, "can agree upon any one thing, it is that the compulsion to move about has created a nation of restless wanderers unlike any other in the world."[2] While he is reluctant to trace this tendency solely to their frontiering heritage, he nonetheless shows that Californians are unusually restless. In 1960 barely one third of them lived in the same house they occupied five years before; northern Californians move about at the rate of one of every three households every year; southern Californians at the rate of one in every two. In the eastern states, by contrast, only one in every ten householders changes residence yearly. Westerners, continues Billington, also apply for 52 per cent more passports than the national average and, in flights between Los Angeles and Chicago, residents of the former city outnumber Chicagoans two to one. "Wandering is a curse for all Americans," concludes Billington, "but doubly so for those who live in the West."[3]

Whatever the relationship between "newness of settlement" and the propensity to change place of residence and to travel, it is a fact that California is predominantly peopled by immigrants from other American states. Indeed, the westward movement of eastern-domiciled Americans is one of the great migrations of modern times. At the 1960 census only 43 per cent of the 15.72 million residents of California had been born in that state, and this percentage includes the California-born children of the immigrants. They had come mainly from the North Central region (3.03

---

[2] *Ibid.,* p. 181.
[3] *Ibid.,* p. 184.

million), the Northeast (1.07 million), the South (2.20 million),
and other states in the West (1.22 million).[4]

There is, however, a great deal of difference between "migratory compulsion" (measured loosely in terms of "frequency of
change in residence within a state" and "frequency of travel
inside the U.S. and overseas") and a decision to settle permanently
outside the United States. The former, as Billington suggests, may
be one legacy of the "pioneer spirit" to which Californians are
closer in time than most other Americans. But how much a
"pioneer environment" influences Californians to leave their homeland for permanent settlement in another country is another question. Research conducted on the motives of emigrants from
northern Europe to Australia suggests that the decision to emigrate is made as a result of the individual's personality and his
perceived dissatisfaction with his social setting.[5] There is no
evidence from studies already conducted among emigrants to
support the proposition that their decisions were, in any way,
heredity-determined (i.e., that they were more likely to be the
children of internal migrants). Research which I have conducted on the motivations of British emigrants to Australia does,
however, indicate that emigrants were more likely to be drawn
from the outer suburbs of cities, usually from semi-detached dwellings in Council estates, than from the high density, poorly housed
parts of the inner suburbs. Many of the emigrants from the outer
suburbs had, however, once lived in the inner suburbs but had
moved out upon marriage. Their emigration to Australia was
really their second migration.[6] Whether emigrants from the

---

4 U. S. Department of Commerce, Bureau of the Census, *U. S. Census of Population: 1960*, Final Report Pc(1)-6D, Detailed Characteristics: California,
Table 98.

5 See A. Richardson, "Some Psycho-Social Aspects of British Emigration to
Australia," *British Journal of Psychology*, Vol. 10, 1959, pp. 327–37; N. H.
Frijda, "Emigrants–Non Emigrants," in G. Beijer (ed.), *Characteristics of Over-
seas Migrants*, Government Printing and Publishing Office, The Hague, 1961;
S. N. Eisenstadt, *The Absorption of Immigrants*, Routledge and Kegan Paul Ltd.,
London, 1954, Chapter 1.

6 R. T. Appleyard, *British Emigration to Australia*, University of Toronto
Press, 1965.

United States are predominantly "second timers," and whether this explains the higher incidence of interest in emigration to Australia by Americans who live west of the Rockies than those who live east (as will be shown in another section of this paper), are questions which require research no less comprehensive than that undertaken in connection with British emigrants to Australia.

Whatever the feasibility of the proposition concerning the Californians' propensity to emigrate farther westward, there is no doubt concerning the increasing number of Americans entering Australia as declared settlers. The number has risen every year since 1959 when only 650 U.S.-born settlers entered Australia; by 1965 the number had reached 2,160. During the same period the number of long-term visitors from the United States (i.e., persons who said on their arrival in Australia that they intended staying for twelve months or longer but had not come to settle) rose from 842 to 2,695 and the annual intake of short-term visitors (i.e., persons who planned to stay less than twelve months) rose from 6,668 to 21,907. Several points of warning should be made concerning the interpretation of these statistics; the first, and most important, being that they are based upon the travelers' *stated intentions.* To the extent that the travelers later changed their minds, e.g., a "long-term visitor" may have decided to stay permanently, the statistics give an inaccurate account of achieved migration. Even the column in Table 1 headed "Net gain" (i.e., the number of persons arriving as declared settlers less the number of former declared settlers who, by definition, changed their minds and departed from Australia), does not necessarily convey the exact position regarding settler gain. Second, Table 1 is based upon arrivals who were born in the United States some of whom may not have been U. S. nationals. Third, not all "former settlers departing" returned to the United States although the majority did.

Despite the difficulties involved in interpreting statistics based on intention, the upward trend of U.S.-born declared settlers entering Australia is unmistakable. Indeed, the United States is the only "providing country" from which numbers have increased every year since 1959. In the financial year 1965–66, U.S.-born settlers comprised 3.3 per cent of all non-British settler arrivals, ranking behind only Italy, Greece, Yugoslavia, Malta, and Germany and ahead of the Netherlands, countries which have been important providers of Australia's postwar immigrants and with which Australia has written bilateral agreements for assisting their nationals with the cost of their outward passages. A more sensitive index of *current* interest in emigration by U.S. citizens is the number of inquiries made concerning opportunities in Australia at the Australian government's several offices in the United States. Until quite recently, the Australian offices in Washington, New York, and San Francisco did not have the facilities necessary to cope with an increasing number of inquiries; many Americans wrote directly to state government offices in Australia, to Commonwealth government offices and the U.S. Embassy in Canberra, and to service organizations such as the Chamber of Commerce in Sydney. Indeed, it was largely because of the diversity of destinations, as well as the rapid increase in the number of inquiries after 1961, that the Commonwealth government decided in 1966 to delegate several officials in their New York and San Francisco offices to the specific task of receiving all inquiries, wherever originally sent.

Prior to the establishment of the Information Offices in New York and San Francisco last year it was not possible to assess the interest shown by Americans in emigrating to Australia. The first reliable estimate was made by the Australian Prime Minister during his visit to New York in July, 1966, soon after the establishment of the Information Offices. Inquiries from would-be settlers, he announced, were running at 2,000 per week. A rate of this magnitude, if maintained, would yield over 100,000 inquiries each year and represent possibly a quarter of a million Americans. Although one needs to know a great deal more about the nature of these inquiries (e.g., how many are "repeats"), it is clear that Australia *is* being considered as a place to settle by a large number of Americans. Equally important is the fact that they *should* be considering emigrating to Australia. And why should the interest have gathered such pace during the last few years? Following an article in the *Reader's Digest* on Australia's potential and a complete issue of the *National Geographic Magazine* on Australia, the response from potential settlers in America was quite remarkable. Would it have been the same had similar articles appeared during the 1950s?

However one chooses to interpret statistics on inquiries about emigration, there is no doubt that the Australian government is taking them, and the consequent increase in settler arrivals, very seriously indeed. Apart from establishing Information Offices in New York and San Francisco, the government's Department of Immigration recently published a booklet, entitled *Australia,* especially for Americans and Canadians who make inquiries about settling in the country.

United States citizens may qualify for assisted passages under the Australian government's General Assisted Passage Scheme. Table 1 shows that in recent years approximately one half of the U.S.-born settlers entering Australia took advantage of this Scheme. Adults receive a subsidy of $160 and children proportionate amounts depending upon their ages. They are not required to repay the subsidy but they are obliged to stay in Australia for at least two years. For the period July, 1963, to June, 1965, statistics are available on the numbers of persons involved in applications for assisted passages received by the Australian Consulates-General in San Francisco and in New York:

	San Francisco	% of Total	New York	% of Total	Total
Number of persons involved in applications for assisted passages	3,507	72	1,342	28	4,849
Number of persons approved for assisted passages	1,115	52	1,049	48	2,164

For our study, the most significant point about these figures is that nearly three quarters of Americans involved in *applications* for assisted passages to Australia applied to the San Francisco office. The majority of them probably lived west of the Rockies and if account was taken of the lower proportion of Americans living in this area, relative to the eastern states, the incidence of interest shown by westerners would be even higher. Before any conclusion could be reached concerning the proportion of Californians among applicants it would be necessary to make a study of the application forms, especially the home addresses of applicants. In the meantime, there is a prima facie case for arguing that interest in Australia's assisted passage scheme is considerably greater among Americans who live west rather than east of the Rockies. Unfortunately, no data are available on the states of residence of non-assisted settlers and, as already noted, these comprise about one half of all settler arrivals during the last few years.

Tables 2 and 3 relating to all U.S. nationals (assisted as well as non-assisted) who entered Australia during 1964–65 as declared settlers, show that they were a very young group (90 per cent were under forty-four years of age) and many were married with young children. In fact, of the 1,139 aged nineteen and over, 711 were married and were accompanied by about 650 children aged eighteen or under. Among single persons aged nineteen and over, males outnumbered females almost four to one. While there is nothing very special about the demographic characteristics of the settlers—these follow the pattern of most free migratory groups—their occupational characteristics are strikingly different from those of other settlers entering Australia. Over 30 per cent of American workers who settled in Australia in 1963–64 were "Professional, Technical, etc. workers" compared with 13 per cent for British nationals, 14 per cent for Dutch and 9 per cent for Germans (Table 3). In addition, they were over-represented in the "Administrative, Executive and Managerial workers" category. Together, these occupation groups accounted for 42 per cent of all American settler workers in 1963–64. Coupled with the steady increase in the total number of declared settlers in recent years, this is the salient feature of immigration from America. It is unusual, too, in that it represents a "brain drain" *from* the United States. The year 1963–64 is by no means unusual. Australia's 1961 census revealed a high proportion of American-born residents in these occupations, although it included persons who were in the country as long-term and short-term visitors. It should, however, be pointed out that U.S.-born settlers in Australia show a greater propensity than any others to change their minds, i.e., to leave Australia as declared "former settlers departing." Exact estimates of loss of U.S.-born settlers are difficult to make from available data. "Settlers arriving" less "former settlers departing" in any one year is a fairly crude measure. The technical problem of "lag" is especially relevant to U.S.-born settlers whose numbers have increased every year since 1959. There is also some "leakage" caused when former declared settlers refuse to describe themselves as such when they return or when they leave Australia within a very short time after arrival and are recorded as "short term departures."

In one sense, i.e., according to estimates of "settlers arriving," Australia has only recently been discovered by Americans. In another sense, however, the two countries have had a fairly close and continuing contact with each other. Contact was first made in 1792 soon after the British government, prevented from sending convicts to the American colonies, chose New South Wales as an acceptable alternative. Hearing at the Cape of Good Hope that the new colony was "in great distress for provisions" the captain of the American brigantine *Philadelphia* returned to the United States, loaded beef, wine, rum, gin, tobacco, pitch, and tar and made for Sydney "for what was probably in his shrewd Yankee mind a promising commercial venture." This blend of American

business enterprise, writes Ian Moffitt,[7] and grudging colonial gratitude opened U.S.-Australian relations, and its element of suspicion
exists today. More than twenty American traders arrived in
Australia's first ten years; American sealers built the first ship in
Australia in 1803–04; Nantucket men commanded most of the
South Sea whalers; two Americans in 1825 were the first foreigners
admitted to citizenship and in 1830 the first American firm established itself in Australia.

Perhaps the most significant event in Australia during the nineteenth century—the discovery of gold—was also the event which
had most effect on relations between the two countries. When news
of its discovery was announced in San Francisco in August, 1851
a rush to Australia began.[8] Probably more than 18,000 persons
arrived in Sydney and Melbourne from America during the five
gold-rush years of the fifties. In 1854 American miners at Bal-
larat, the scene of one of the biggest discoveries, formed a
guerrilla corps called The California Rangers to take part in fighting, if it began, to create an Australian republic. But unfortunately
(for Australia), writes Jonathan Gaul, gold was discovered in
Peru shortly afterwards and most of the Americans were gone
before the famous battle at Eureka Stockade.

In the following hundred years immigration from America was
reduced to a trickle although the influence of American ideas and
methods was considerable. The most significant contact during
this period was made between 1941 and 1945 when over 1,120,000
American troops were embarked for service in the South West
Pacific,[9] and probably more than 750,000 of them saw some
service in Australia. After the war some 12,000 Australian brides
of U.S. servicemen went to the United States and, in much smaller

---

[7] In a series of articles in *The Australian* last year.

[8] Jay Monoghan, *Australians and the Gold Rush. California and Down Under 1849–1854,* University of California Press, 1966, p. 198.

[9] Chester Wardlow, *U. S. Army in World War II,* The Technical Services, The Transportation Corps; Movements, Training and Supply. "Troop Move-ments to the Overseas Commands," Chapter 2.

numbers, U.S. servicemen settled in Australia. From the end of the war until the 1960s the number of "permanent and long-term" arrivals in Australia from the United States averaged about a thousand a year. It is only since then that numbers have increased significantly, as shown by Table 1. Why this should have occured only recently is hard to answer although the reasons given by some Americans presently in Australia as to why they emigrated throw some light on the problem.

It must be emphasized that even under academically acceptable interview conditions the motives of emigrants are difficult to assess. They invariably rationalize the logic of their decisions and try to convey that their dissatisfaction with their social setting was so great that emigration was the only solution. Even so, recent research on the motivations of British, Dutch, and Greek emigrants to Australia suggest that economic dissatisfactions and the hope for better opportunities and higher real income in the proposed country of settlement are the main determinants of modern, free migrations. During the 1950s, when real income differentials between these countries and Australia were wide, emigration was considerable. The reduction of these differentials during the past five years has, in the case of Holland, reduced emigration to a trickle and there is certainly not the same compulsion among Greeks to emigrate overseas as there was during the 1950s.

If real income differentials still determine the direction and the volume of free migration, why should people be emigrating, in increasing numbers, from the wealthiest country on earth to one where real incomes are a great deal lower for most occupations? In the absence of basic motivation research, we simply don't know and many of the suggestions put forward in the following pages are very speculative indeed.

During the last two years I have read hundreds of letters, addressed to government departments and service organizations, from Americans who were interested in settling in Australia. The majority were from young college graduates, executives, and small investors: a licensed pilot-cum-contractor from New Mexico who sought "opportunities for going into business myself" and who had listed a dozen questions about housing finance, schools, and whether he could bring his trucks and autos; a young man from California who was completing his B.Sc. in Business Administration and who declared, "I'll come right to the point—I've been considering moving to Australia after completing school"; a graduate from California who wanted details of jobs for librarians and who "hoped eventually to make his home in Australia after graduation and marriage"; a veterinarian from Colorado who owned a sheep property and had $200,000 to invest. In discussing what little we know about the motives and the experiences in Australia of people like these it does seem useful to divide them into two groups, the "farmer investors" and the "wage earners," if only because the economic basis of decision-making by members of each group seems to be quite different.

The Colorado sheep breeder may well have shared the views of an Arizona cattleman who, when interviewed on his new cattle property in North Queensland said he wanted to "get back to the frontier country; they were closing in on me (in Arizona)." But, commented the journalist who interviewed him, ". . . behind the move there is more than a sentimental desire for open spaces. In a beef-short world, the Americans have shrewdly assessed the enormous potential of (Australia's) backward northern pastoral country." It has been estimated that the entry of a small number of experienced Americans into the tropical north Queensland pastoral industry could, with U.S. capital and the introduction of new techniques, increase the area's carrying capacity by five- to tenfold.

Nowhere in Australia has the impact of American settlers, with their capital and "know how," been more dramatic than in the cotton industry which they virtually began in the Namoi valley near Narrabri, New South Wales. Last summer, the valley's twenty-five Californian families harvested 28,000 acres of cotton.

In 1959, prior to the arrival of the Americans, only ninety-seven acres were under cotton in all Australia. How did the Californians come to dominate the industry? It all began in 1961 with the arrival of Paul Kahl and Frank Hadley from Merced, California, on a twelve-day trip to "study conditions." Once they decided that the Namoi valley was ideal country for growing cotton they returned to California, sold up, and returned to commence farming their first sixty-five acres of cotton. Why did they leave California? Paul Kahl, a fourth-generation Californian whose great grandfather walked across the Panama Isthmus to join the California Gold Rush, put it this way: "We were under a continuing squeeze in California as to acreage and net income. Acreage controls on cotton were getting tighter and tighter. This left the position of trying to expand rather difficult. We were looking elsewhere . . . and we heard about Australia. We heard from a couple of sources that the Australian government wanted cotton grown and, in fact, was paying a subsidy." The guarantee offered by the Australian government was forty cents per pound for five years which was seven cents per pound higher than the current California price. The success of Kahl and Hadley attracted other Californians—from Merced, McFarland, Clovis, Porterville, Fresno, and Chico—now there are twenty-five Californian families there, a total of 109 persons. Their contribution to the industry is not simply their output of cotton but the way they operate. Wee Waa, the small town that services the valley, suddenly found new branch offices of five major farm-equipment companies to service the equipment of the newcomers. For each family has invested approximately $100,000 in land and equipment necessary to grow cotton in such a large way. The Californians not only brought new ideas and modern equipment to the area but they also attracted twenty-nine Australian families who, themselves, have for the first time become growers of cotton.

One of the most successful Californians, however, has been Marvin Amaro, a former potato and cotton grower from Fresno who, in less than twelve months, became the largest tomato grower in New South Wales. Like Paul Kahl, he also came to "look around." "After six months," he said, "I was satisfied that in Australia there was a future for us and I went back to the States to bring my family to Griffith (New South Wales)." They arrived in July, 1965, and by April, 1966, had harvested 3,500 tons of tomatoes for the local canneries and many more tons for the vegetable markets in Sydney, 400 miles away. In addition, he grew 130 acres of cotton, 80 acres of rice, sorghum and carrots.

Farmers like Kahl and Amaro succeeded not simply because of their "drive" but also because they had the capital necessary to apply techniques and equipment to industries in Australia which had never seen their like before. Whether they and their compatriots left the United States solely because of the restrictions there on production of cotton is conjectural. Their decisions, like those of most emigrants, were probably reached after a serious weighing of their economic and social setting in the United States relative to their expectations of economic achievement in Australia.

But what of the individual American wage earner—the college graduate, the professional, the craftsman—who leaves his homeland with only modest capital and is obliged to find a place in established Australian industry in competition with Australian workers? The pity is that we know practically nothing about their motives for emigrating or their achievements in Australia. There is some evidence that the decisions of many wage-earners especially young, single workers, are made on the basis of their wanting "to look around for a year or two"; in such cases they are hardly being "pushed" out of the United States by perceived inadequacies in their social setting. High rates of return by Americans, for example, suggest that there may be a large number of such "trippers" in the settler component of American arrivals. On the other hand, many of the wage earners were probably very serious about their perceived inadequacies of American society but they too returned to the United States because they could not find suitable employment in Australia or because Australian society did not measure up to their expectations. Problems of finding suitable employment could very well apply to professional workers, especially those in professions which, in Australia, demanded British degrees.

The few American wage earners in Australia who have discussed their decisions to leave America emphasized "choked cities," "racial integration policies," and "government controls" as inadequacies in their social setting. Some of them also invoked their "pioneering spirit" as the reason why they had reacted so drastically against their social setting. This is not quite as implausible as it sounds. I have already referred to the research of Richardson and Frijda on the motives of emigrants from northern Europe to Australia. Richardson, a social psychologist, discovered that, relative to a control group of non-emigrants from the same social setting, British emigrants whom he studied had rather different personality characteristics. They were more likely to have feelings of anxiety and show greater responsiveness to their environment than non-emigrants. Frijda, by using a similar technique, showed that intending Dutch emigrants were more ambitious, more motivated, and more interested in action and in hard work than were non-emigrants. So it would seem that emigrants probably have rather different personality types than their compatriots and this could apply to Californians as well as Britons.

One seldom hears an American in Australia saying that he emigrated because of poverty, need, and "lack of opportunities" in his homeland. This is not the case with other migrants. For example, 63 per cent of a sample of British emigrants to Australia in 1959 stated that "better opportunities for themselves and their children" was their main reason for leaving Britain.[10] Many of these emigrants were professional workers and craftsmen who had reckoned, in terms of real income and opportunities for advancement, that they would be better off in Australia. Follow-up interviews conducted with the same persons in Australia during the

---

10 R. T. Appleyard, *op. cit.*, p. 165.

following seven years showed that they were better off than they had been in Britain or, probably, were better off than if they had never emigrated. A similar study among workers leaving Greece in 1964–65 showed that the "economic motive" was even more dominant in decision-making: "poverty in Greece," "desire for a steady job," "hope to own a business"—conditions and aspirations which largely reflect differential real incomes between Greece and Australia.

In view of the high real incomes for most occupations in America, high, that is, relative to other countries, it is hardly surprising that there should be little or no reference to the "economic motive" by Americans who have settled in Australia. Indeed, it is quite likely that the majority of Americans who have settled in Australia recently actually experienced a decline in real income. If this is so, the basis of their decisions to emigrate is quite atypical of all known non-refugee migrations in modern times. Perhaps Australia offered them some non-economic attraction (climate, "way of life" . . .) which they considered more important than economic betterment, or the inadequacies of their social setting in America were so great that they were prepared to accept lower real incomes in order to avoid them.

Predominant amongst the reasons given by some Americans for emigrating have been "the Negro problem" and "the hopelessness of living in high-density, cluttered cities." The two are not unrelated. Americans who have clearly disagreed with integration policies and said that Australia was a logical place to settle mainly because it had very few colored people and an immigration policy which restricts their entry, usually find Australians quick to emphasize that they do not want their country to become a haven for racists. Recently an American schoolteacher emigrated to Australia because, he said on arrival, he disagreed with "forced integration" in schools there. The then Deputy Leader of the Opposition (Mr. E. G. Whitlam) raised this case in the House of

Representatives by asking the then Minister for Immigration (Mr. H. Opperman) what attitude his Department took towards prospective migrants who proclaimed their view of Australia as a racial refuge. The Minister gave a very politic reply:

> I would say that the inquiries made regarding people who are migrating from countries such as the United States would cover security, character, general background and fitness to be in this country. I would not imagine that personal views such as those mentioned by the honourable member would be canvassed. Perhaps it is unwise for people to express extreme views, but I should think that the views expressed from time to time by honourable members on the other side of the House are far more extreme than any views held by (the American schoolteacher).

Politic though the reply may have been, the possibility of Australia becoming a racial refuge as a result of "white backlash" in the United States is one of the disturbing aspects of what otherwise appears to be considered by Australians as a welcome migration.

But whether or not Australia's restrictive immigration policy, and its legacy of an almost homogeneously white population, is a dominant factor in the decisions of some Americans to settle there, the policy itself will sooner or later become a key issue in the future of American emigration to Australia. The policy clearly discriminates against colored persons. Semi- or unskilled American Negroes are in exactly the same position, vis-à-vis emigration to Australia, as semi- or unskilled Asians, Africans, and other non-Europeans. Recent changes in the administration of restrictive immigration policy allowed for the intake of a small number of non-Europeans, although successful applicants are required to be highly skilled and be able to speak English. In announcing the changes, the Minister for Immigration emphasized that they were not intended, as is immigration from European countries, to meet "general labour shortages." What this amounts to for American

Negroes is that a truck driver would almost certainly not be admitted for permanent settlement but a Dean Dixon (conductor of the Sydney Symphony Orchestra) would.

So far, Australia has avoided the difficulties which such a policy clearly foreshadows by negotiating assisted passage agreements only with countries in Europe with basically white populations. Despite the growing importance of the United States as a provider of settlers, an assisted passage agreement has never been written with that country. If it did, the open rejection of a Negro applicant for assistance simply because of his race would come against U. S. federal legislation outlawing such discrimination. The U. S. government would be in a very difficult position if it condoned a policy under which Australia agreed to assist white but not Negro applicants with similar qualifications. Until now, the Australian government has cleverly avoided the issue by assisting white Americans under the provisions of its "General Assisted Passage Scheme," a kind of residual scheme covering persons from countries with which no bilateral agreement has been made. U.S. nationals have comprised 20 per cent of all arrivals under the G.A.P.S. since 1960.

There is plenty of evidence to show that Negro organizations in the United States are not unaware of Australia's policy. During the Australian Prime Minister's visit to New York last year a protest was organized by a militant wing of the civil rights movement against Mayor Lindsay's official dinner in the Prime Minister's honor. Their protest was based on Australia's immigration policy, especially its restriction on the entry of Negroes. Then, following a visit to Australia last year, Era Bell Thompson, the Negro writer, made a strong attack on the policy: "By using race or color as a criteria puts her on the side of the bigot whom a white man's country attracts and who is a deterrent to peace, brotherhood and assimilation of non-white people into white communities all over the world." Straws in the wind maybe, but both events signify the basic problem which has to be solved before assisted immigration from the United States to Australia can be placed on a firm, official footing.

I have dwelt at length on the Negro question not because I believe it has dominated the motives of Americans who have emigrated to Australia but simply because it is the major problem in the future of migration between the two countries. If, as suggested, the prospect of immediate economic betterment is relatively less important in the decisions of American emigrants than it is in the decisions of Britons and Greeks, other dissatisfactions with American society than the Negro problem may also figure prominently. Peter Michelmore, writing from New York, wrote of ". . . tired cities, overcrowded schools, choked highways, polluted waterways, recklessly expensive doctors and a government that cannot cope" as contributing to the decisions of American emigrants. Without a systematic study on motivations it is not possible to assess their respective influence, if any, on individual decisions. The implication, of course, is that Australia has *relatively* lively cities, empty highways, clean waterways, cheap doctors, and a government that can cope and that prospective emigrants know this. Both propositions need a lot of investigation. I think a social researcher, for example, might have to travel some distance before he found an Australian who agreed with this description of his country's services, even in terms relative to America's. It would also be necessary to investigate the influence of close political ties, especially in foreign policy, between the countries, the fact that English is the spoken language in both countries and, as Michelmore reflects, the similarity ". . . in habit, material possession and worldly attitude." The researcher may well find that prospective settlers' knowledge of Australia is very limited and that their decisions had been based upon quite erroneous information like the family who, with others, intended to buy a large motor cruiser to sail to Australia with implements and seeds and who wrote to the

Department of Immigration asking them to recommend a bay where they could anchor safely while building their homeland on virgin soil.

In the final analysis it must be asked whether a wage earner can be satisfied in a country, whatever its non-economic attractions, if his real income is lower than in his homeland. Wage earners generally live well up to their incomes and any decline in income as a result of migration requires them to make substantial readjustments. When interviewed in Australia last year, several California wage earners, who were about to return to America, gave this advice to their countrymen: "If you come to Australia with less than $20,000, have a round-trip ticket. But if you have money, this can be a commercial paradise." Both the proposition and the advice would need to be carefully examined; there is some evidence, however, that they may have been echoing the experiences of many of their compatriots in Australia.

It has not been possible to explore very far the validity of the proposition that Californians, and their children, closer than other Americans to the frontier, are more likely than easterners to emigrate to Australia. Even with reliable data the proposition is really too broad and too dependent upon answers to other basic questions to be adequately answered, or answered at all. The limited data at our disposal has indicated that emigration from the United States to Australia is not only increasing but that residents living west of the Rockies have shown a greater propensity than those living in eastern states to apply for assisted passages to Australia. Nothing at all is known of the state of residence of non-assisted settlers to Australia whereas these comprise about half the current flow. The other firm conclusion we can reach is that American settlers to Australia (both assisted and non-assisted) are predominantly young single persons or young families and, relative to Australia's occupation structure, are over-represented in the "Professional" and "Executive" groups.

Because motivation research is such a difficult field, requiring the application of academically acceptable interview techniques—procedures which could not be adopted for this article—comments which have been made on why Americans are emigrating to Australia and what happens to them after they arrive there are very speculative indeed. The few interviews which have been conducted with Americans in Australia suggest that they could be conveniently divided into two main groups: "farmer investors" and "wage earners." Californian cotton growers are one example of the former group. They claim to have been "pushed" out of their state by unjust laws on the production of cotton although they did not leave until they discovered that Australia provided the facilities for continuing as cotton growers. With large amounts of capital, and "know how," they virtually pioneered the industry in Australia. Cattlemen from the western states of America have, with capital and experience, also made a major contribution to the cattle industry in northern Australia but their "migration" appears to have been based largely on the economic prospects that this industry offered.

Very little is known about the wage-earning emigrants; why they left America and what happened to them in Australia. It appears that many of them left America for what have been loosely described as "non-economic" motives—dissatisfactions with policies covering racial integration and with problems associated with living in high-density areas. Whether the high rate of return among American settlers relative to other migrant groups is partly because Australian society did not measure up to their expectations, or whether it reflects the great adjustment which has to be made when one's real income declines, is uncertain. These and other questions on the remarkable increasing emigration of American settlers to Australia deserve a great deal more attention than has been accorded them in this chapter.

TABLE 1

Migration Statistics: U. S. Born to Australia

| | U.S. Born "settlers" | | | | | U.S. Born "long-term visitors" | | | U.S. Born "short-term visitors" | | |
| | Settlers arriving | | | Former settlers departing | Net gain | Arrivals | Depar-tures | Net gain | Arrivals | Depar-tures | Net gain |
	Assisted	Other	Total								
1959	343	307	650	98	552	842	452	390	6,668	6,937	—269
1960	451	395	846	111	735	1,084	676	408	8,445	8,651	—206
1961	477	463	940	142	798	1,264	654	610	10,926	11,169	—243
1962	381	656	1,037	230	807	2,013	881	1,132	12,666	13,151	—485
1963	568	625	1,193	357	836	1,753	802	951	15,088	15,990	—902
1964	781	724	1,505	406	1,099	2,106	1,129	977	18,137	18,706	—569
1965	1,055	1,105	2,160	500	1,660	2,695	1,681	1,014	21,907	22,895	—988
1966*	886	770	1,656								

* To September 1966.

Source: Commonwealth Bureau of Census and Statistics, Canberra.

Note: A "settler" is a person who, on arrival in Australia, states that he has come intending to settle.
A "long-term visitor" is a person who, on arrival in Australia, states that he intends to stay for twelve months or longer but not settle.
A "visitor" is a person who states, on arrival, that he intends to stay for less than twelve months.

TABLE 2

United States Nationals—Settler Arrivals
by Age and Conjugal Condition, 1964–65

| Age Groups | Males | | | Females | | | Total | % |
	Single	Mar-ried	Widowed and Divorced	Single	Mar-ried	Widowed and Divorced		
0–18	359	—	—	305	2	—	666	36.9
19–24	119	37	5	30	74	4	269	14.9
25–44	142	248	29	39	210	11	679	37.6
45–64	10	95	11	6	41	14	177	9.8
65 and over	—	4	2	1	2	5	14	0.8
Total	630	384	47	381	329	34	1,805	100.0

TABLE 3

Settler Arrivals by Nationality and Occupation, 1964–65

Category	U.S.A.		British		Dutch		German	
	No.	% of Wkrs.	No.	% of Wkrs.	No.	% of Wkrs.	No.	% of Wkrs.
Professional, Technical, etc. Workers	249	30.6	5,177	13.0	152	14.3	187	9.5
Administrative, Executive, and Managerial Workers	92	11.3	1,758	4.4	50	4.7	39	2.0
Clerical Workers	98	12.0	5,760	14.5	136	12.8	245	12.5
Sales Workers	61	7.5	2,292	5.8	67	6.3	89	4.5
Farmers, Fishermen, Hunters, etc.	32	3.9	1,013	2.5	28	2.6	33	1.7
Miners, Quarrymen, and Related Workers	1	0.1	386	1.0	7	0.6	8	0.2
Workers in Transport and Communications	41	5.0	3,136	7.9	54	5.1	70	3.6
Craftsmen, Production-Process Workers	152	18.7	14,309	36.0	349	32.7	976	49.6
Laborers	11	1.4	2,130	5.4	52	4.9	104	5.3
Service and Sport Workers	40	4.9	2,276	5.7	83	7.8	135	6.9
Not Stated	37	4.6	1,506	3.8	88	8.2	82	4.2
Total Workers	814	100.0	39,743	100.0	1,066	100.0	1,968	100.0
Number of Dependents	991		50,717		1,209		1,274	
Total Settlers	1,805		90,460		2,275		3,242	

Workers as Percentage of Set

NOTES ON CONTRIBUTORS

R. T. Appleyard is Professor of Economic History at the University of Western Australia, Nedlands. In 1955 he was awarded a Population Council Fellowship at Duke University, where he attained the M.A. and Ph.D. degrees. He is the author of *British Emigration to Australia* (University of Toronto Press).

John Bright is a Hollywood screen writer and novelist, long a resident of Southern California.

Jennifer Cross is a free-lance writer living in Berkeley.

James P. Degnan teaches creative writing at the University of Santa Clara; his stories and articles have appeared in *Atlantic, Esquire, Commonweal,* and other publications.

Howard F. Gregor is Associate Professor of Geography at the University of California (Davis) and the author of *Environment and Economic Life* (Van Nostrand).

Gladwin Hill, who has covered Southern California for *The New York Times* for many years, heads the *Times* Los Angeles bureau. He has recently completed a book on California politics.

Robert Kirsch has published several novels; he is literary editor of the Los Angeles *Times.*

Richard G. Lillard teaches at California State College (San Fernando) and is the author of *Desert Challenge, The Great Forest,* and *Eden in Jeopardy* (all published by Knopf).

D. B. Luten is Lecturer in Geography at the University of California (Berkeley); his particular concerns are with the interaction of populations with national resources and the rise of the conservation movement.

Wesley Marx is a free-lance journalist living in Southern California. His most recent book is *The Frail Ocean* (Coward-McCann).

Theodore Roszak formerly taught history at California State College (Hayward), served as editor of *Peace News* (London) and edited *The Dissenting Academy* (Pantheon).

James Schevill, poet and playwright, is director of the Poetry Center at San Francisco State College. His most recent book is a collection of three plays, *The Black President and Other Plays* (published by Alan Swallow).

Art Seidenbaum, columnist on culture for the Los Angeles *Times,* was former West Coast editor for *The Saturday Evening Post* and former Los Angeles correspondent for *Life.*

Scott Thurber is on the staff of the San Francisco *Chronicle.*

Mel Wax is Public Affairs Director of KQED in San Francisco.

Samuel E. Wood is Executive Director of California Tomorrow, a nonprofit educational organization dedicated to bringing to the public a greater awareness of the problems involved in maintaining a beautiful and productive California; he is one of the editors of *Cry California.*